BLACK FLY STEW

Simple Gourmet Lamb

with Side Dishes & Wine Pairings

KATE KRUKOWSKI GOODING

Northern Solstice Publishing, LLC

Sage n' Sophie, Kate and Don, lamb and wine … all heavenly pairs.

NORTHERN SOLSTICE PUBLISHING
PO Box 991
Mount Desert, ME 04660

KATE KRUKOWSKI GOODING
Black Fly Stew: Simple Gourmet Lamb with Side Dishes and Wine Pairings

ARTWORK
Cover art by Russell D'Alessio
Cover and book design by KAT Design, LLC

Inside Art and photography work by:
Russ D'Alessio, www.rdalessio.com
Jan Leudolph, John Warnick
Kate Krukowski Gooding www.blackflystew.com

Spices and some descriptions compliments of
The Spice House www.thespicehouse.com
Wine descriptions taken from my testing notes; from several wine purveyors,
www.winesearcher.com, and reference books;
What to Drink With what you Eat, and *The Wine Bible*.

ISBN 978-1-60585-686-5

This cookbook is dedicated to you, the cooks in the kitchen!

ACKNOWLEDGEMENTS

Thank you testers, your participation and important feedback from testing the recipes is an invaluable part of this process: Devorah Rifka Barlock, Marc Bergeron, Sue Ellen Bordwell , Anne Bossi, Patty Puiia Cobb, Dr. Stephen Curtin, Don Gooding, Leslie Edwards Huméz, Suzi and Todd Foster, Nancy J. Hill, Marjorie Love, Samantha Lundgren, Catherine McKinney, Paul and Julie Pampinella, Michelle Panars, MaryAnn Perlman, Allison Ponce, Francine Schrock, Deke Sharon, Anne Abbe Smith, Shaun Stuart, Deborah Tucker, Sandra Wilcox, Catherine Woodward, and Brittany Young.

I feel fortunate to work with many specialty food providers and use their products in my cookbook: Bob Bowen and Anne Bossi (Sunset Acres Farm and Dairy, Brooklin, ME), Karen Raye (Raye's Mustard, Eastport, ME), George Stone (Maine Goodies, Albion, ME), Patty Penzey Erd (The Spice Company, Chicago, IL), and Tim Ziter (Sweet Energy, Colchester, VT).

Many thanks to the many wine aficionados who worked with me to provide some wonderful wine suggestions for these lamb dishes: Daniel Bridgers (Maine Distributors, Bangor, ME), Scott Worcester (Sawyer's Specialties, Southwest Harbor, ME); Nicole Taliaferro (DaVine Wines, Bowdoinham, ME), Jack Scully (Easterly Wines, Belfast, ME), and Marc Bergeron (Vinifera Imports, Ltd., Stoughton, MA). And to two outstanding Maine wineries: Bob and Kathe Bartlett (Bartlett Maine Estate Winery and Spirits of Maine Distillery, Gouldsboro, ME), and Tod and Treena Nadeau (Dragonfly Farm and Winery, Stetson, ME).

Special thanks to cover artist, Russ D'Alessio, who as a nationally recognized artist, reflects his undeniable passion for life in all his paintings. I am grateful to have his talent grace my cookbook covers. And to my friend Kat Stuart, whose graphics design talent showcases my ideas into this resulting cookbook.

PREFACE

This cookbook, *"Simple Gourmet Lamb with Side Dishes and Wine Pairings,"* allows you to create an entire meal that you, your family, friends and guests can all enjoy. True, I do love to cook; however, I do not want to be in the kitchen all day. So the dishes are not complicated where you need to be in the kitchen for two days to prepare a meal, and they allow you to use many ingredients that are already in your pantry.

Lamb has been a favorite of mine for many years. When I was living in the city and couldn't satisfy my taste for game meat, lamb did it for me. It is not a mild meat and has some prominent game flavor unless it is totally grass-fed, which I only discovered a few years ago when visiting a girlfriend who moved to Oregon to raise them. She cuts her own grass to feed them throughout the winter – it's a lot of work but well worth the effort. The flavor was so mild and delicious - I love it! Here in Maine our local grass-fed lamb purveyor is my friend Bob at Sunset Acres Farm and Dairy. Find out who is your local purveyor and give them a try. Your guests will leave with a palatial pleasurable smile, and you'll hear about it for a long time.

The gaminess of grain-fed lamb is a problem for some people, and while I enjoy both grain- and grass-fed varieties, many of the recipes in this book, like the game recipes in my first cookbook "*Wild Maine Recipes,*" will make converts out of people who never liked it before. One of the pleasures of cookbook writing is connecting with friends who test the recipes before they go to print. When I received feedback from testers for this cookbook, I was happy to hear that a number of previous lamb avoiders thoroughly enjoyed the recipes. Who do you know that you can convert?

I have been cooking ever since I can remember, but pairing food with wine began when I started managing restaurants and needed to create wine lists that would pair with the restaurant menu. I went very quickly from white Zinfandel to Chablis, red Burgundy, red Zinfandel and then Cabernet Sauvignon. My friend Margot used to tease me that when I discovered big California cabs, I craved that explosive nose, chewy body and tantalizing tannins so much, I was hard to persuade to try anything else. Now I have mellowed to white Burgundies, Pinot Noirs and the oldest Ports I can find, but continue to explore Malbecs, Riojas and many more of the literally thousands of different wines from around the world. Ever a student, I have learned from restaurateurs, wine purveyors, oenophiles (a fancy word for wine connoisseurs that I can't pronounce) and friends.

Within the pages you will see what grapes pair well with certain lamb dishes and their unique combinations and layering of herbs and spices, as well as what spices combine to make an uncanny wonderful finish on your tongue. What does your palate tell you? Listen to what your eyes see, your nose smells, and your mouth tastes to decide what wines you enjoy.

As you peruse these pages remember the wine suggestions in this cookbook are just that, suggestions. Embark on a journey to your local wine store and ask questions to expand your wine horizon. Let them know what you enjoy drinking now and what dish you will be matching. Specialty wine shops carry a wide variety of wines from all over the world; they vary in costs, and are available both corked and uncorked (some of the best wines in our cellar have screw caps!). Ask if they have wine tastings, as this is the perfect opportunity for you to learn what else you might enjoy.

I remember one night our friend Kim had come over and we had pulled out some nice reds to enjoy with dinner. She immediately said not to waste them on her, that she wouldn't know the difference. My husband Don immediately replied that she should give her palate some credit and try the red, which was a very nice California Cabernet Sauvignon. Kim now understands there are differences and you can tell what they are if you take the time - and a coach always helps too! She is now a red wine convert and has many favorites. Remember to just give yourself a chance to expand what you already know and enjoy.

Combining great food, great wine, great friends – it's a magic I first encountered as a young student able to afford only an artist's rendition. I was looking to fill my walls at college, and there it was, encased in a soft yellow matt frame staring up at me from the pile of prints (I still have it!). Auguste Renoir's masterpiece "Luncheon of the Boating Party" has been a driving force behind my increasingly interesting social meals ever since. With soft brushstrokes he evokes a harmony of food, wine, friends and setting. To me his painting represents the ultimate social engagement of friends gathering, sharing conversation, food and wine. I strive for this feeling of presence, for me and for our guests, as I plan and prepare for each and every get-together.

Above all, the one thing I tried to achieve in this cookbook was to recommend grapes and wines that could bring the wine and lamb dish in harmony, to better enable a Renoir-like gathering. This is difficult given all the variables involved: type and cut of lamb, spices, cooking technique, and most importantly individual tastes. We all have our own particular palates, and keeping that in mind I hope you enjoy your travels through my cookbook, into your local lamb and wine shop and back to your kitchen! Bon Appetit!

Contents

Braised Lamb au Jus Syrah
with Roasted Rosemary Maine Potatoes 12

Braised Lamb Shanks in a Reduced Fig, Zinfandel
and Balsamic Sauce with a Sweet Potato Mash 14

Braised Lamb Shanks and Orange Zest
with Brown Buttered Noodles 16

Breaded Romanian Lamb Loins with Beet Salad 18

Broiled Lamb Kebabs in Yogurt Sauce with Indian Rice Pilaf 20

Burgundian Lamb Stew with Provencal Flatbread 22

Caribbean Lamb 26

County Cork Irish Stew 28

Creole Lamb on French Bread 30

Crown Roast of Lamb with Saffron Rice..............................32

Curried Lamb Stew 34

Day Ahead Greek Lamb Stew...36

Greek Grilled Lamb with Mediterranean Rice Pilaf 38

Grilled Lamb with Potatoes and Rosemary Chimichurri..........40

Grilled Rack of Lamb with Aleppo Chili Balsamic
   Glaze, Sweet Potatoes and Steamed Broccoli 42

Indian Grilled Lamb with Lacha...44

Jamaican Jerk Lamb Chops with Sweet Yam Mash 46

Jamaican Spiced Lamb with Rasta Rice 48

Lamb and Artichoke Stew with Baked Rice 50

Lamb and Morels with Asparagus.......................................52

Lamb Chops with Saffron Orzo...53

Wicked Good Lamb Chops in a Balsamic Marinade
   with Baked Potato Wedges 54

Mustard Crumb Wrapped Lamb with Grilled Asparagus 56

Lamb Roast with Curry Sauce and Garam Masala Rice 58

Lamb-Stuffed Sweet Peppers 61

Contents *continued*

Lamb with Blueberry Shallot Sauce and Glazed Carrots 62

Maine Maple Braised Lamb Chops with Ambercup Squash 64

Marsala Morel Mushrooms over Grilled Lamb
    with Baked Potato Wedges 66

Mediterranean Lamb with Squash and Saffron Couscous 68

Mediterranean Lamb, Sausage and Orange Slices
    with Mushroom Pilaf 70

Mexican Lamb Chili 72

Mexican Lamb Roast with Vegetable Rice 74

Mongolian Lamb and Noodle Salad 76

Moroccan Spiced Lamb with Balsamic Vinaigrette Salad 78

Moussaka 80

Mustard-Crusted Lamb Salad with Blue Cheese
    and Fig Balsamic Vinaigrette 82

Parmesan Kalamata Encrusted Lamb
    with Braised Cremini Mushrooms 84

Pomegranate Lamb, Chestnuts and Apricots over Saffron Rice . . . 86

Porcini Encrusted Lamb Chops with Sweet Pepper
    and Asparagus Rice Salad 88

Roast Lamb Shoulder Provencal with Anise Carrots 90

Roasted Spicy Bordeaux Lamb Leg with Sweet Onion
    and Cheddar Bake..92

Rosemary Lamb Roast with
    Portabella Sauce and Goat Cheese Polenta 94

Spicy Island Lamb 97

Spanish Lamb with an Apricot Glaze,
    Couscous and Asiago Carrot Patties..............................98

Spicy Lamb Meatballs with Garlic Peanut Sauce Appetizer 100

Spicy Stir-Fried Sichuan Shredded Lamb with Soba Noodles ... 102

WINE DESCRIPTIONS and PURVEYORS..........................104

Braised Lamb au Jus Syrah with Roasted Rosemary Maine Potatoes

I grew up on ketchup. It seems we ate it on almost everything. I was literally forced into trying mustard at Disneyland when I ordered a burger and it came with the works: ketchup, mustard and a pickle. Was I going to pick it off in front of my girlfriend, me, who will try anything? Well I ate it, I enjoyed it, and now I search for the ultimate mustards for sandwiches, salads, salamis, pretzels (Amanda - they need Dijon for NYC pretzels?!) and fingers!

Since I found Raye's in Eastport, Maine, I have found their abundance of flavors and textures satisfy me, and my cooking demands, on so many levels.

6	1-pound lamb shanks
	Salt and freshly ground pepper
4	tablespoons extra virgin olive oil, divided
3	carrots, coarsely chopped
2	celery ribs, coarsely chopped
2	cups onion, coarsely chopped
1	tablespoon tomato paste
2	cups Syrah or other hearty red wine
1	bay leaf
6	whole Malabar black peppercorns
4	cups chicken stock
1	cup *(packed)* flat-leaf parsley leaves, finely chopped
2	teaspoons finely grated lemon zest
4	garlic cloves, minced

PREHEAT oven to 300°F. Season the lamb shanks with salt and pepper. Heat 2 tablespoons olive oil in a large cast iron casserole. Working in batches, cook the lamb shanks over moderate heat, turning often, until well browned on all sides, about 12 minutes; transfer to a platter. Pour off any fat from the casserole and add the remaining 2 tablespoons of olive oil.

ADD carrots, celery and onions and cook over moderate heat until the vegetables start to brown, about 8 minutes. Stir in tomato paste, and then add the wine, scraping up the browned bits from the bottom. Stir in the bay leaf and peppercorns. Return the lamb shanks to the casserole and add the stock. Bring to a boil, cover and bake the shanks in the oven for 3 hours. Transfer shanks to platter and remove the meat from the bones. Put the meat in a bowl and cover with damp towel.

STRAIN the sauce into a large saucepan, pressing on the vegetables to extract as much liquid as possible. Boil the sauce over high heat until it is thick enough to coat the back of a spoon, about 25 minutes; season with salt and pepper. Return the lamb to the sauce and rewarm over moderate heat. In a small bowl, mix the parsley with the lemon zest and garlic. Spoon lamb on warm dish aside roasted potatoes, sprinkle with zest and serve.

1   pound Maine potatoes, scrubbed, dried and chunked
1   pound sweet potatoes, scrubbed, dried and chunked
2   tablespoons Raye's Garlic Honey Wine mustard
2   tablespoons extra virgin olive oil
3   sprigs of fresh rosemary, stripped and chopped
    sea salt and fresh ground pepper

PREHEAT oven to 375°F. Non-stick cooking spray an 11" x 13" baking dish.

COMBINE mustard, olive oil, and chopped rosemary in a large bowl. Add chunked potatoes and toss to coat thoroughly. Transfer coated potatoes to baking dish and generously sprinkle with sea salt and pepper. Roast for 45 minutes or until tender and nicely browned. Turn potato chunks halfway though. (*Serves 4*)

WINE: *Rhone or Syrah/Shiraz*

Braised Lamb Shanks in a Reduced Fig, Zinfandel and Balsamic Sauce with a Sweet Potato Mash

I tested this recipe one night with my husband, Don, and our friends, Scott and Jennifer Worcester of Sawyer's Specialty Wines and Sips Restaurant. Scott brought 4 bottles of wine covered in numbered wrappers; blind tastings can be so much fun! I was amazed by the results. The winner was a 1989 Bartlett's Blueberry Reserve Wine with a 1997 Chateau Masar from Lebanon as the runner up. Do not be influenced by past myths of fruit wines being all fruit, sweet and unpalatable with anything but desserts. This blind tasting proved to us all that Bartlett's 1989 Blueberry Wine stood its ground against some of the best wines from France, Lebanon and California.

4	1-pound lamb shanks
1	teaspoon salt
1	teaspoon Indonesian Lampong black peppercorns* freshly crushed *(young, spicy black peppercorn)*
½	cup flour
¼	cup canola oil
2	cups onion, chopped
4	garlic cloves, chopped
12	dried figs, quartered
1	cup red Zinfandel wine
½	cup Zinfandel port
½	cup Tawny Port
½	cup balsamic vinegar
3	juniper berries, slightly crushed
2	cups chicken stock
1	cup lamb *(or beef)* stock
2	tablespoons fresh rosemary, chopped

PREHEAT oven to 325°F.

SEASON shanks with salt and pepper and then dredge in flour. Heat oil on medium high in stockpot until smoking hot; add shanks and brown all sides well. Transfer shanks to plate. Reduce heat to medium and add onion and garlic; sauté until fragrant, about 1 minute. Add figs, red Zinfandel wine, ports, vinegar and juniper berries and cook over medium heat until reduced by half, about 10 minutes. Add stock and bring to a boil for 3 minutes. Remove from heat, add lamb shanks and rosemary, stir, cover pot with lid and place in oven to cook for 2 hours.

REMOVE pot from oven and place shanks on a warm plate tented with aluminum foil; reserve liquid for the sauce. On medium heat, reduce sauce until thick enough to coat the back of a spoon, about 10 minutes. Ladle sauce over the shanks and serve hot.

2	large sweet potatoes, baked
1	cup chicken stock
½	cup onion, chopped
3	tablespoons apple cider vinegar
2	tablespoons butter
1	teaspoon salt

PREHEAT oven to 350°F. Spray small baking dish with non-stick cooking spray.

SCRAPE baked sweet potatoes out of skin; set aside in medium bowl. Heat chicken stock in small saucepan and add onions, cook for 2 minutes on high heat. Add apple cider vinegar, butter and salt; stir for 1 minute. Combine onion mixture with sweet potatoes in bowl; slightly blend with immerser or potato masher, leaving some onions visible.

POUR sweet potato mixture into baking dish; bake for 30 minutes. (*Serves 4*)

> **WINE:** *red Zinfandel. We had a 1989 Bartlett's Blueberry Reserve and 1997 Chateau Musar (Lebanon, rich in character and unusual in style).*

*COOK'S NOTE Indonesian Lampong black peppercorns add a little heat to any dish. Available at www.thespicehouse.com.

Braised Lamb Shanks and Orange Zest with Brown Buttered Noodles

Sometimes I want a more complex flavor and brown butter offers it up for me. I love it on broccoli. Brown butter is made by cooking the butter long enough to turn the milk solids and salt particles brown while cooking out any water.

8	1-pound lamb shanks
	kosher salt and freshly ground pepper
2	tablespoons olive oil
2	carrots, chopped
1	medium onion, coarsely chopped
1	bottle dry red wine
2	28-ounce cans Italian peeled tomatoes with their juice
4	cups chicken stock or canned low-sodium broth
20	garlic cloves, peeled
4	bay leaves
2	cinnamon sticks
8	flat-leaf parsley sprigs plus 1 tablespoon minced parsley
1	tablespoon finely grated orange zest

PREHEAT oven to 325°F. Season the lamb shanks generously with salt and pepper.

HEAT olive oil in large cast-iron casserole. Brown lamb shanks thoroughly over moderately high heat, turning often, about 3 minutes per side; transfer the shanks to large bowl; cover.

ADD carrots and onion to casserole and cook, over moderately high heat, stirring occasionally, until browned, about 5 minutes. Add wine and boil for 5 minutes; scrape up browned bits from bottom of casserole.

RETURN lamb to casserole. Add tomatoes, chicken stock, 20 garlic cloves, the bay leaves and cinnamon sticks. Tie parsley sprigs with string and add them to casserole. Bring to boil, then cover and cook in the preheated oven for 1 1/2 to 2 hours, or until lamb is tender.

12	ounces egg noodles
6	tablespoons butter
4	garlic cloves, minced
1	cup Asiago cheese, grated

MEANWHILE cook and drain noodles, pour into large bowl, and cover to keep warm.

REMOVE casserole from oven. Transfer lamb shanks to large bowl and cover with foil. Discard cinnamon sticks, bay leaves and parsley. Puree vegetables. Strain sauce back into casserole through sieve. Boil sauce until reduced by half, stirring frequently, about 30 minutes. Season with salt and pepper and return the lamb shanks to the sauce and simmer to heat through.

MEANWHILE in a small bowl, combine minced parsley and orange zest; set aside.

IN a large saucepan melt 6 tablespoons butter on medium-high heat. When butter bubbles subside, add garlic and stir. Cook 2 minutes. When butter turns copper colored, immediately pour over noodles and toss with Asiago.

ON warm plates place buttered noodles, spoon sauce over meat, sprinkle with the zest mixture and serve. (*Serves 8*)

> **WINE:** *Bordeaux from the Medoc Region, Cabernet Sauvignon or Pinot Noir. We enjoyed a 1996 Wente Reliz Creek Reserve Pinot Noir; with its spicy oak, raspberry overtones and solid tannins, it was a good match for this earthy, full-flavored lamb.*

Breaded Romanian Lamb Loins with Beet Salad

I remember the first time I ever ate beets, and it was in a salad. It was fall of 1979. I had just finished working three months for Hans, owner of the Hotel Alpina in Arosa, Switzerland. I had a week before I was meeting my boyfriend in Wiesbaden, Germany; Joey had bought tickets to see Supertramp in Frankfurt as a birthday present. Astrid, a part timer, asked if I would watch her two children in Lugano for a week while she and her husband took a vacation. Absolutely! I heard Lugano was beautiful and it would be fun to explore.

The afternoon I arrived, Astrid was making a simple beet salad to go with cold chicken. It was delicious. I tried to remember exactly how she did it and put my little twist on it. (p.s. the concert was amazing!)

6	red beets, stems and root ends removed
½	cup red onion, sliced very thin
2	tablespoons olive oil
2	tablespoons balsamic vinegar
¾	teaspoon mustard powder
½	teaspoon thyme
	salt and freshly ground black pepper
4	ounces goat cheese

PREHEAT oven to 400°F. Wrap each beet in foil.

ROAST beets until soft, about 1 hour. Cool slightly; remove foil. Rub off skins; cut into wedges. Combine oil, vinegar, mustard powder and season with salt and pepper; toss and set aside.

12	one-inch lamb loin chops
3	tablespoons extra virgin olive oil
1½	teaspoons roasted ground cumin, divided
1	tablespoon chopped fresh thyme

    2   garlic cloves, peeled and crushed
    2   eggs, lightly beaten
    1   cup Panco bread crumbs for dredging
        salt and black pepper to taste
    ½   cup dry white wine
        chopped fresh parsley leaves for garnish *(optional)*
    2   lemons cut into wedges, for serving

PLACE loin lamb meat between sheets of wax paper and pound to
½ inch thickness with rolling pin. Heat oil in nonstick skillet over
medium-high heat; add 1 teaspoon cumin, thyme, and garlic.
Discard garlic cloves when oil begins to shimmer. Dip lamb into
egg, press into bread crumbs on both sides and add to skillet;
brown about 2 minutes per side. While lamb is cooking, sprinkle
remaining cumin, salt and pepper. Lamb should remain rare.
Transfer lamb to a warm plate and tent with aluminum foil.

DRAIN oil from pan leaving the browned bits; add wine to pan and
scrape bits into the wine. Allow the mixture to simmer until
reduced by half, 3 to 5 minutes.

DIVIDE lamb among 6 plates, top with parsley and serve wine sauce
and lemon wedges on the side. Sprinkle cheese on top of beets and
serve. *(Serves 6)*

WINE: *white Burgundy such as Macon-Villages, California
unoaked Chardonnay or a red Burgundy.*

Broiled Lamb Kebabs in Yogurt Sauce with Indian Rice Pilaf

2   pounds boneless lamb shoulder or leg,
    cut into 2-inch chunks
3   red or yellow bell peppers
3   fresh Anaheim or other mild chilies
1   onion, peeled and cut in half
2   tomatoes
    salt and black pepper to taste
1   teaspoon fresh thyme leaves or a pinch of dried
2   cups plain yogurt
    lemon wedges for serving

PREHEAT broiler and adjust the rack so it is about 4 inches from the heat source.

HEAT a cast-iron skillet, or other heavy skillet, on high. Add the lamb and quickly sear on all sides. Don't worry about cooking it thoroughly; brown the exterior well, about 5 minues.

REMOVE lamb and put the peppers and chilies in the same skillet at high heat. Add onion, cut sides down. Cook until peppers blacken on all sides, turning as necessary *(onion will blacken quickly; remove and set aside)*. When peppers begin to collapse, about 15 minutes, remove skillet from heat and cover with foil.

REMOVE cooled peppers from the pan; peel and seed them, then cut or tear them into strips. Separate the onions into rings. Cut the tomatoes in half and over a sink squeeze to extract the seeds. Put the tomatoes, cut side down, in the skillet and char them, 3 to 5 minutes; roughly chop the tomatoes.

COMBINE the vegetables with the lamb, salt, pepper, thyme, and yogurt in a roasting pan just large enough to hold the lamb in one layer. Broil until charred on top, just a few minutes, then serve over rice (see below) and with lemon wedges.

Indian Rice Pilaf

1½	cups basmati rice
2¼	cups chicken broth
1½	teaspoons salt
½	teaspoon black pepper, ground
3	tablespoons unsalted butter
1	cup onion, chopped
2	garlic cloves, chopped
2	teaspoons ginger, minced
⅛	teaspoon cinnamon
⅛	teaspoon cardamom, ground
2	tablespoons currants, chopped
2	tablespoons parsley, chopped

BRING chicken broth to boil, add salt, pepper and rice and cook for 10 minutes or until done. Meanwhile, sauté onion and garlic in butter for 1 minute. Add ginger, cinnamon, and cardamom and cook 1 more minute. Add cooked rice, currants and parsley and stir. Let stand 5 minutes then serve. (*Serves 6)*

WINE: *Beaujolais-Villages, Barbera or full-bodied Pinot Noir (French, California or Oregon).*

Burgundian Lamb Stew with Provencal Flatbread

When my husband began to test this recipe he announced, in a frustrated voice, that he was already 2 hours behind from when he wanted to begin. For me, that was a red flag understanding his patience level, as anyone's, can diminish. I abandoned my cookbook editing and took the cats for a walk. I had just rounded the corner of the garage when I heard, "KATE!" Well needless to say I didn't get very far on my walk and stayed to close to home to, rightfully, clarify some of his other questions.

This exercise is always good for me to repeat. I learn that there is much I take for granted (yes you need to put the bread in a bowl to rise and not just cover it with a damp towel) and I need to clarify directions if someone who is not a regular in the kitchen is to get great results for the recipe.

2	pounds lamb stew meat
¼	cup finely chopped fresh flat parsley
2	tablespoons fresh thyme, finely chopped
2	tablespoons fresh rosemary, finely chopped
2	tablespoons fresh sage, finely chopped
2	tablespoons extra virgin olive oil
2	teaspoons salt
2	tablespoons canola oil
1	large onion, coarsely chopped
1	carrot, chopped
4	garlic cloves, chopped
1	tablespoon Herbes de Provence*
2	cups white Burgundy wine
2½	cups chicken broth, divided
1	tablespoon butter, room temperature
2	teaspoons all-purpose flour
½	cup chicken broth
2	teaspoons ground black pepper
2	15.5-ounce cans Cannellini Beans

STIR parsley, thyme, rosemary, and sage in medium bowl to blend. Add olive oil and mix until herbs are sticking together. Salt lamb, then add to herb mixture and toss; marinate 30 minutes. Meanwhile start the Provencal Flatbread *(see below)*.

HEAT oil in large stockpot on medium-high; add lamb and sauté until browned; remove and set lamb aside. Sauté onions, carrot, garlic and Herbes de Provence for 5 minutes. Add lamb and juices, wine, 2 cups of chicken broth and simmer, covered, for 2 hours.

COMBINE butter and flour to a paste. In small saucepan, whisk paste into ½ cup broth then simmer sauce until slightly thickened; 1 minute. Stir into stew until thoroughly combined. Add beans and simmer 20 minutes. Serve hot with Provencal Flatbread. *(Serves 8)*

Provencal Flatbread

1	cup warm water
1	tablespoon sugar
1	envelope dry yeast
3	tablespoons olive oil, divided
2½	cups white flour
1	teaspoon dried rosemary
1	teaspoon lavender
1	teaspoon salt
1	tablespoon fresh rosemary, chopped
1	garlic clove, chopped
1	teaspoon sea salt

PREHEAT oven to 400°F.

MIX water, sugar and yeast in mixer bowl, let dissolve for 5 minutes. Stir in 2 tablespoons oil, flour, rosemary, lavender and salt. Add more flour if needed. Knead on dough hook about 8 minutes. Place dough in bowl, let rise 1 hour in warm place with a covered damp towel.

HEAT remaining tablespoon oil in small sauce pan on low heat, sauté fresh rosemary and garlic for 2 minutes.

PUNCH dough down and roll out on lightly floured surface to about 1 inch thickness, brush on rosemary oil and then sprinkle with sea salt. Place on heated stone in oven and bake on bottom rack for 15-20 minutes.

Herbes de Provence
You can buy it or use my recipe.

1 tablespoon dried basil
1 tablespoon marjoram
1 tablespoon summer savory
1 tablespoon thyme
1 teaspoon crushed bay leaf
1 teaspoon lavender
1 teaspoon fennel

WINE: *white Burgundy, unoaked Chardonnay, Soave, Nebbiolo, or Syrah.*

COOK'S NOTE Brush more olive oil on crust when it comes out of oven for a softer top.

Summer Savory

Caribbean Lamb

Did you know that chilies are the second most common spice and food, after salt, used in the world? They are very prevalent in many cultures; the Scotch Bonnet is from Jamaica. Chilies are becoming more common here as diverse cultures bring their culinary preferences to the U.S. In many cases we devein and deseed the chili peppers before we cook or eat them. The veins contain a substance called capsaicin that causes the heat of chilies and peppers. It is a flavorless, odorless chemical concentrated in the veins of chilies and peppers.

I first tried Scotch Bonnet peppers in Montego Bay at The Pork Pit (great, very casual outside place that is no longer there). They had a hot sauce for Jerk Chicken or Pork, as if it is not already hot enough. I loved it! I had plenty of tears, hydrated my contacts and grabbed a Red Stripe Beer to cool my mouth.

½	cup curry powder
2	large sprigs thyme
1	Scotch bonnet peppers, finely chopped *(or jalapeno peppers)*
1	onion, diced
3	scallions, diced *(reserve some greens for garnish)* salt and freshly ground black pepper
2	tablespoons olive oil
2	pounds lamb roast, bone in
¼	cup chopped fresh garlic
1	carrot, diced
1	tomato, diced
½	pound potatoes, diced
¼	cup chopped ginger
1½	quarts chicken stock

TO MAKE the marinade, combine the curry, thyme, Scotch bonnets, onion, scallions, salt, and pepper. Rub lamb with spices and marinate lamb overnight. Remove the lamb from the marinade, reserve leftover marinade.

SEAR lamb over high heat in olive oil in a large cast iron pan. Add garlic, carrot, tomato, potatoes, ginger, and reserved marinade and stir to combine. Add stock and simmer for 1 ½ hours or until meat is tender and about to fall off the bone.

REMOVE the meat from the casserole and place on a warm platter and tent with aluminum foil. Return pan to stove over medium-low heat and cook until sauce has thickened. Top roast with vegetables and sauce and garnish with scallions. (*Serves 6 to 8*)

WINE: South African Warwick Pinotage, a Vouvray, a California Chapellet Chenin Blanc or a Red Stripe beer here!

County Cork Irish Stew

Irish stew is a hearty, flavorful peasant dish typically made with the least expensive and sometimes older cut of lamb (aka sheep or mutton), and readily-available ingredients (potatoes, onions and parsley). The Irish raised primarily sheep and root crops, and potatoes were the main food crop prior to the potato famine. Even though I have not been in contact with my relatives from County Cork, I am tipping my hat to their old tradition.

My niece Tracy is in County Cork as I write. After graduating from Culinary Arts, she was awarded a George Mitchell Peace Scholarship to a Culinary School in Ireland. I am sure I will get a different take on this recipe once she returns! Her mom, Anne, tested this recipe for me, and said "ditch the cheesecloth because it's good luck to the one who finds the bay leaf in their stew." And she added, "we served Guinness Beer especially since 2009 is the 250th anniversary of the Guinness Beer Brewery."

1½	pounds lamb stew meat
	salt and pepper to taste
2	tablespoons fresh chopped parsley
1	bay leaf
1	teaspoon peppercorns
1	teaspoon thyme
1	teaspoon rosemary
1	tablespoon canola oil
2	cups lamb, game or beef stock
4	potatoes, peeled and chopped
1	medium onion, chopped
1	sweet onion, chopped
2	leeks, white only, sliced thin
5	carrots, sliced
2	tablespoons roux *(equal parts butter and flour)*
	parsley for garnish

SALT AND PEPPER lamb meat. Wrap chopped parsley, bay leaf, peppercorns, thyme and rosemary in cheesecloth.

HEAT oil in stockpot and brown meat on all sides and add stock. Bring to boil; add herbs in cheesecloth and simmer for one hour on low.

ADD potatoes, onion, leeks and carrots and simmer another 30 minutes. Remove cheesecloth and stir in roux. Simmer 15 minutes more. Garnish with parsley and serve with crusty bread and a pint. *(Serves 4)*

WINE: *Bordeaux, Cabernet Sauvignon or a Guinness Beer! Specifically we liked a Chateau Margaux and an Italian Barbaresco with this dish.*

Here is a picture of Anne's mom, and Tracy's grandmother, Sue Abbe, enjoying Irish Stew with a Guinness Beer in a local pub upon their arrival in County Cork April 2009!

Creole Lamb on French Bread

Have you ever wondered how the names were derived for some things, drunken goat cheese being one of them? This cheese originates from the village of Jumilla in the Murcia region of Spain. It is a semi-soft artisan goat cheese with a smooth violet rind which has been soaked in Doble Pasta wine for 48-72 hrs. It is aged for about 75 days, resulting in a sweet, smooth flavor. Drunken goat cheese used to be difficult to find, thank goodness not anymore!

2   tablespoons olive oil
1   medium red onion, chopped
1   yellow bell pepper, seeded chopped
2   tablespoons Creole spice mix *(see recipe at right)*
1   pound lean ground lamb
4   French bread rolls, halved
4   slices drunken goat cheese
     (or soft goat cheese to spread)
     Dijon mustard

PREHEAT grill to high.

HEAT the oil in a large nonstick skillet over medium-high heat. Add onion, pepper, and Creole spices. Sauté until vegetables are soft, about 5 minutes. Remove from heat and let cool for 10 minutes.

COMBINE cooked vegetables with ground lamb in a large bowl. Form into shaped patties *(same size as rolls)*. Grill 4 minutes per side, or until no longer pink in the center. Place burgers on rolls and top with mustard and cheese. *(Serves 4)*

Creole Spice Mixture

3 tablespoons sweet paprika
2 tablespoons kosher salt
2 tablespoons garlic powder
1 tablespoon black pepper
1 tablespoon onion powder
1 tablespoon cayenne powder
1 tablespoon oregano
1 tablespoon thyme
1 tablespoon sweet basil

COMBINE all ingredients and store in glass jar.

WINE: *Cerasuolo, from Sicily, a Rhone/Provence Rose or a sparkling off-dry Riesling Spatelese. We tried a 2003 Warwick Cape Ladies red table wine from South Africa. It was soft with a medium round body that was just plain luscious in your mouth and went great with this dish.*

Crown Roast of Lamb with Saffron Rice

Sauce

- 1 tablespoon unsalted butter
- 1 small red onion, peeled and diced small
- ¾ cup dry red wine
- ¼ cup red wine vinegar
- ⅓ cup apricot preserves
- ⅓ cup roughly chopped fresh spearmint
  kosher salt and freshly cracked black pepper to taste
- 2 tablespoons butter

MELT butter in medium sauté pan, over medium heat. Add onion and cook, stirring occasionally, until translucent, about 7 to 9 minutes. Add wine, vinegar, and preserves and simmer until the sauce is reduced to about 1 cup, 35 to 40 minutes. Remove pan from heat, add the mint and butter, and season with salt and pepper.

Saffron Rice

- 1 tablespoon unsalted butter
- ½ teaspoon saffron *(about 20 threads)*
- 1 tablespoon ground coriander
- 1 small red onion, peeled, halved, and thinly sliced
- 1½ cups long-grain white rice
- 3 cups chicken stock
- ¼ cup sliced almonds, toasted in a dry skillet over medium heat, 3 to 5 minutes
- 3 tablespoons chopped fresh parsley
  kosher salt and freshly cracked black pepper to taste

PREHEAT oven to 500°F.

MELT butter in a medium sauce pan, over medium heat. Add saffron, coriander, and onion and cook, stirring occasionally, until the onion is translucent, 7 to 9 minutes. Add the rice and stir to coat with the oil, and then add stock. Bring to a simmer, cover; reduce the heat to low, and cook until all the liquid has been absorbed, 15 to 18 minutes. Stir in the almonds and parsley and season with salt and pepper. Cover the pan with a tea towel, put the lid on, and set aside.

Crown Roast of Lamb

- 1 lamb rib crown roast* *(2 racks of lamb, about 1 pound each, frenched and tied in a crown shape)*
- 2 tablespoons olive oil
  kosher salt and freshly cracked black pepper to taste
- 2 tablespoons minced garlic
- 2 tablespoons freshly cracked coriander seeds *(or 1 tablespoon ground coriander)*
- ½ cup roughly chopped fresh parsley

COMBINE olive oil, salt and pepper, garlic, coriander and parsley for marinade. With a brush, baste half on lamb racks. To keep crown shape, place an oven proof bowl in the middle of the crown.

COVER the bones with foil at the top to prevent burning. Place in shallow roasting pan and bake for 15 minutes. Reduce heat to 325°F. Baste lamb with remaining marinade. Allow to cook an additional 5 minutes for medium-rare or check every 5 minutes for desired doneness. Let set for 5 minutes to rest. Rewarm the sauce, slice 3-4 chops per warm plate, serve with saffron rice and top with sauce. *(Serves 4 to 6)*

WINE: *Primitivo di Manduria from Puglia or a CA red Zinfandel.*

***COOK'S NOTE** A crown lamb roast is two racks of lambs tied together to create a crown! You can also bake this recipe with ribs lying down and not crowned. A grass-fed lamb rack usually weighs about 1 pound, other lamb racks can be heavier. Adjust seasoning accordingly.

Curried Lamb Stew

I love the flavor of this Maharajah curry powder that The Spice House, yes, hand makes. They describe it as "a beautiful, rich, sweet curry, perfumed with fragrant cardamom powder that they grind themselves from the inner seeds of the green cardamom pod. This elegant curry powder also flows with the rarest of all spices, genuine Spanish saffron. In addition to the golden hue that saffron brings to a dish, its unique flavor cannot be imitated. A little of this curry powder goes a very long way. Hand mixed from: turmeric, coriander, cumin, cardamom, fenugreek, ginger, nutmeg, fennel seed, Chinese cinnamon, white pepper, arrowroot, black pepper, ground cloves, cayenne pepper and superior grade Spanish saffron."

1½	pounds lamb stew meat, shoulder cut into 1½ inch pieces
1	cup sliced onions
1	tomato, seeded and chopped
1	teaspoon chopped fresh ginger
3	garlic cloves, crushed
1	tablespoon Maharajah curry powder*
	salt and freshly ground pepper
1	tablespoon ghee* *(or canola oil)*
¼	cup water
½	teaspoon hot sauce *(Sambol style sauce)*
2	potatoes, peeled and diced
2	carrots, sliced
4	scallion stalks, thinly sliced for garnish

PREHEAT oven to 350°F.

IN a large bowl, combine lamb with onions, tomato, ginger, garlic, curry powder, and salt and pepper to taste. Mix well and marinate in the refrigerator overnight.

REMOVE meat from marinade, reserve marinade. In a large stockpot, over moderately high heat, brown meat in ghee until golden brown on all sides. Pour any excess fat from pot. Add reserved marinade and hot sauce and sauté for 6 minutes. Return meat to pot with enough water to just cover the meat and bring to a boil. Cover and put pot in the oven for 1 ½ hours. Add potatoes and carrots to the pot, return pot to oven and cook for 40 minutes or until meat is tender. Serve with scallions on top. *(Serves 4)*

WINE: *Alsatian, Pinot Blanc or a chilled red Zinfandel. Two of my favorite red Zinfandel's for this dish are from California: Chateau Montelena and Brown Vineyards.*

*COOK'S NOTE Maharajah curry powder is available from The Spice House, online at www.thespicehouse.com. Ghee is a solid clarified butter; it heats without burning at a high temperature.

Tomatoes

Day Ahead Greek Lamb Stew

We know that soup always tastes better on the second day, so why not make it ahead? Although Brittany, my tester, said it smelled so good she just couldn't wait. And she said it was good the next night too!

There are a few types of oregano. This Greek oregano has a bright, sweet flavor and a clean lemony overtone that blends well with most Mediterranean dishes.

¼ cup olive oil
1½ pounds boneless lamb chuck cut into 1½-inch cubes
2 tablespoons flour
1½ cups onions, chunked
2 cups tomatoes, peeled, seeded, and chopped
3 garlic cloves, minced
1½ teaspoons dried thyme
1 teaspoon dried rosemary
1 teaspoon Greek oregano *(or regular oregano)*
½ teaspoon lavender
1 bay leaf, crumbled
2 cups dry red wine
½ pound feta cheese, crumbled
salt and freshly ground pepper

PREHEAT oven to 350°F.

HEAT oil in heavy 5-quart stockpot over medium high heat. Toss lamb with flour in large bowl. Add lamb in batches and cook until browned, stirring occasionally. Transfer lamb to bowl when cooked.

ADD onions to pan and cook until light brown, stirring frequently, about 5 minutes. Add tomatoes, garlic, thyme, rosemary, oregano, lavender, and bay leaf; stir in wine and lamb, bring to a boil. Cover and bake in oven for 2 hours. Cool and refrigerate for the next day or two.

PREHEAT oven to 350°F. Let stew stand at room temperature while oven is heating.

HEAT stew for 90 minutes. Stir feta cheese into stew and return to oven; bake uncovered until cheese has heated through, about 10 minutes. Season with salt and pepper to taste and serve. *(Serves 4)*

WINE: *Argentinian Malbec or a sparkling Shiraz. We had a Lidakis (Greek dry medium-bodied red),*

Oregano

Greek Grilled Lamb with Mediterranean Rice Pilaf

1   3-pound leg of lamb, deboned and butterflied
4   fresh thyme sprigs
6   fresh rosemary sprigs
4   garlic cloves
     zest of 1 orange
1   teaspoon black pepper
½   teaspoon kosher salt
3   tablespoons olive oil

PREHEAT gas grill on high.

TRIM the lamb of any excess fat and, if any parts seem overly thick, make a horizontal cut in the meat so they lie fairly flat. Strip the thyme and rosemary leaves from the stems and mince. In a bowl combine with garlic cloves, orange zest, pepper, salt and oil. Use a thinbladed knife to poke some holes in the lamb and stick a little bit of the mixture into each of them; then rub the meat with the remaining herb mixture. Marinate at room temperature for 30 minutes. *(Meanwhile, start soaking rice – see below).*

GRILL the lamb until it is nicely browned, even a little charred, on both sides, 20 to 30 minutes, and the internal temperature at the thickest part is about 125°F. Let rest for 5 minutes before slicing, as you would a thick steak.

Mediterranean Rice Pilaf

¼   cup ghee
1   onion, finely chopped
2   garlic cloves, crushed
2   cups long-grain rice, washed, soaked in cold
     water for 30 minutes and drained

8	ounces button mushrooms, wiped clean and chopped
1	teaspoon salt
½	teaspoon black pepper
4	cups hot chicken stock
1	bay leaf
⅛	teaspoon lemon zest
1	cup kalamata olives, pitted and slightly chopped

MELT ghee in sauce pan on medium high heat. Add onion and garlic, sauté 5 minutes. Add rice, stirring constantly for 5 minutes. Add mushrooms, salt and pepper; stir constantly for 4 minutes. Add stock and bay leaf and bring to boil. Reduce heat, cover and simmer for 20 minutes or until all liquid is absorbed.

REMOVE mushroom pilaf from heat. Remove bay leaf, stir in lemon zest. Spoon pilaf on warmed serving platter and scatter olives on top. Serve immediately. *(Serves 6)*

WINE: *Rioja, Barbera or full-bodied New Zealand Pinot Noir.*

Kalamata Olives

Grilled Lamb with Potatoes and Rosemary Chimichurri

1¼ cups extra-virgin olive oil
½ cup rosemary leaves, finely chopped
1 head of garlic, minced
  zest and juice of 1 lemon
½ teaspoon crushed red pepper
  kosher salt
1 2-pound boneless lamb roast, butterflied
  freshly ground black pepper
8 tablespoons unsalted butter
5 large sweet potatoes, peeled and sliced ¼-inch thin
2 tablespoons olive oil

PREHEAT two ovens* to 500°F.

COMBINE oil, rosemary, garlic, lemon zest, lemon juice, crushed red pepper and 1 tablespoon kosher salt. *(This marinade is best made 2 days ahead and refrigerated).*

SEASON lamb with salt and pepper and brush ½ cup of rosemary marinade on both sides. Set the lamb aside, fat side up, on a large rimmed baking sheet and roast in the upper third of the oven for about 25 minutes, or until an instant-read thermometer inserted in the thickest part of the meat registers 125°F for medium rare. Transfer lamb to cutting board, cover with foil and let rest for 10 minutes. Lamb will continue to cook and keep juices inside.

TOSS potatoes with remaining rosemary marinade. Transfer herbed potatoes (without excess marinade) to a baking sheet and season with salt. Bake for 20 minutes, turning once. Thickly slice lamb. Arrange potatoes on warmed plates, top with lamb. *(Serves 6)*

WINE: Aglianico, Cabernet Sauvignon, or a Gigondas.

*COOK'S NOTE If you do not have two ovens, cook potatoes first then cook lamb. While lamb is resting under foil tent place potatoes back in oven for 5 minutes to warm.

Rosemary

Grilled Rack of Lamb with Aleppo Chili Balsamic Glaze, Sweet Potatoes and Steamed Broccoli

I discovered Aleppo chili pepper while I was doing a cookbook tour at The Spice House in Chicago. Patty and Tom were most gracious hosts and put up with my curiousity and questions. Of course I am sure they were happy when I left with (REALLY) a suitcase full of spices. And Aleppo chili pepper was one of them.

The chili pepper comes to us from northern Syria, near the town of Aleppo, which is considered one of the culinary meccas of the Mediterranean. It has a moderate heat level with some fruitiness and mild, cumin-like undertones. It has a very robust flavor that hits you in the back of your mouth, tickles your throat and dissipates quickly.

2	teaspoons whole fennel seeds
	juice of 1 blood orange
2	garlic cloves, mashed
2	tablespoons olive oil
1	tablespoon Aleppo chili pepper, ground *(or 2 teaspoons crushed red pepper flakes)*
1	2 - 2½ pound rack of lamb
2	teaspoons salt
¼	teaspoon black pepper
¾	cup balsamic vinegar
¼	teaspoon Aleppo chili pepper, flaked *(or crushed red pepper flakes)*
½	tablespoon rosemary, finely chopped
2	sweet potatoes
3	cups broccoli

TOAST fennel seeds in cast iron pan over low heat until fragrant, about 2 minutes, cool and grind. Whisk together fennel, juice, garlic, olive oil and chili pepper. Place rack of lamb in baking pan and cover with marinade. Cover with plastic and marinate overnight.

PREHEAT grill to high. Spray grills with non-stick cooking spray. Preheat oven to 375°F.

BAKE sweet potatoes in oven for 1 hour.

REMOVE lamb from refrigerator 30 minutes before grilling and season both sides with salt and pepper; reserve marinade. Meanwhile prepare glaze. Combine balsamic vinegar and chili pepper in small saucepan over high heat. Reduce by half, about 4 minutes. Remove pan from stove, add rosemary and stir.

PLACE lamb on grill, fat side down. Grill lamb until fat begins to caramelize, about 5-7 minutes. Turn lamb rack over and grill another 5 minutes. Remove and brush reserved marinade on both sides. Grill lamb for 20-25 minutes for medium-rare (internal temperature 125°F), or longer if desired. Steam broccoli for 7-10 minutes.

DIVIDE lamb on four warmed plates with balsamic vinaigrette glaze on top and sweet potato and broccoli on the side. *(Serves 4)*

WINE: Pinot Noir. We had a Cellardoor Vineyards Prince Valiant with intense aromas of ripe black cherries and white pepper with undertones of coffee and caramel.

Indian Grilled Lamb with Lacha

Lacha is a raw onion salad. In India, many dinners are accompanied by a raw dish and/or chutney. I like using lots of sweet onions in this dish.

- 12   1-inch lamb rib chops *(not tiny riblets)*
- ¼   cup water
- 3   tablespoons canola oil
- 2   tablespoons curry powder
- 1   tablespoon white vinegar
- 2   teaspoons onion powder
- 1   teaspoon garlic powder
- 2   teaspoons Garam Masala *(see recipe at right)*
- 1   teaspoon salt

PLACE lamb chops in a shallow baking dish. Combine remaining ingredients and pour over chops. Cover and refrigerate for 3 hours.

Lacha

- ¾   cup sweet onions, halved and sliced thin
- 1   plum tomato, halved and sliced thin
- 1   tablespoon fresh mint leaves, chopped
- ¼   teaspoon salt
- ¼   teaspoon black pepper
- ⅛   teaspoon cayenne pepper
- 1   teaspoon lemon juice

COMBINE all Lacha salad ingredients and mix well. Refrigerate at least 3 hours before serving. This allows flavors to infuse.

PREHEAT grill on medium high. Oil grill racks (or use non-stick spray) before cooking.

PLACE chops on grill and cook for 2 minutes per side for medium rare, or until desired doneness. Remove from heat and serve with Lacha. *(Serves 6)*

Garam Masala

1   tablespoon cardamom seeds
1   teaspoon whole cloves *(Penang)*
1   teaspoon whole black peppercorns *(Tellicherry)*
1   teaspoon whole black cumin seeds
2   inch stick cinnamon
⅓   of whole nutmeg
½   teaspoon coriander
½   teaspoon mace

COMBINE and grind in spice grinder, store in glass jar.

WINE: *Beaujolais-Villages, Chablis, or red Zinfandel.*

Mint

Jamaican Jerk Lamb Chops with Sweet Yam Mash

Thank goodness for testers with adventurous friends. Shaun tested this recipe three times on her frinds, and once using pork chops. The heat was definitly Jamaican.

2 yams, baked
1 teaspoon sweet paprika
1 teaspoon dark brown sugar
½ teaspoon ginger
½ teaspoon salt
¼ teaspoon black pepper
¼ teaspoon thyme
⅛ teaspoon cayenne
2 tablespoons butter

SCRAPE yam out of skin and mash.

COMBINE paprika, brown sugar, ginger, salt, black pepper, thyme and cayenne. Add spices and butter to mashed yams and stir until combined.

Jamaican Jerk Sauce

2 garlic cloves, with skin on
¼ cup lime juice
¼ cup dark brown sugar
1 teaspoon Scotch bonnet pepper, deseeded and chopped *(or jalapeno)*
2 scallions, green and white, sliced
½ cup onion, minced
1½ tablespoons ginger, minced
½ teaspoon thyme, dried
⅛ teaspoon allspice, ground
8 1-inch lamb chops

TOAST garlic in cast-iron pan over medium heat until blistered on all sides; about 8 minutes. Peel and mince garlic. Combine all ingredients together, except lamb. Rub lamb chops with jerk sauce and marinate at room temperature for 1 hour, turning once.

PREHEAT oven to 450°F.

REMOVE lamb from marinade and pat dry, reserve marinade. Heat oil on high in cast-iron pan until shimmering; add lamb and sear over moderately high heat until nicely browned, about 2 minutes on each side.

PLACE lamb on a rimmed baking sheet. Roast in the upper third of the oven for 15 minutes. Let lamb rest 5 minutes before serving on warmed plate; serve Jamaican Jerk Sauce on the side with Sweet Yam Mash. *(Serves 8)*

WINE: *chilled red Zinfandel, Primitivo or Red Stripe Beer. We enjoyed a 2003 Brown Estate Chiles Valley red Zinfandel.*

Jamaican Spiced Lamb with Rasta Rice

Rasta or Rastaman conjures up visuals of dreadlocked, laid back Jamaicans who are all about enjoying life in their own way. They are unlike the newest group called Rastas: a mysterious gang of dreadlocked fugitives who live deep in the Congo forest, wear shiny tracksuits and Los Angeles Lakers jerseys, and have a notorious reputation. The fashion statement is quite the image for the Congo jungle!

Paul and Julie are Boston-based cooks, who enjoy lots of beans. They suggested two cans of black beans instead of one. It added to the taste, texture, color and overall presentation of the dish.

¼   cup crushed pineapple
2   tablespoons canola oil
6   scallions, chopped
4   garlic cloves, minced
1   Scotch bonnet pepper, seeded and chopped
1   tablespoon dark brown sugar
2   teaspoons kosher salt
1   teaspoon cinnamon
1   teaspoon ground allspice
2   teaspoons fresh thyme *(or 1 teaspoon dried thyme)*
6   1½-inch lamb loin chops *(or center cut leg lamb chops)*
2   tablespoons olive oil
¼   cup cilantro, chopped

COMBINE first ten ingredients and food process until it resembles a paste. Rub paste lightly on both sides of lamb and marinate in refrigerator at least 3 hours.

HEAT olive oil in a large cast iron skillet. Add chops and cook over high heat, about 3 minutes per side for medium-rare. Transfer lamb to plates, add rice *(see recipe at right)* and garnish with the cilantro and serve.

Rasta Rice

1   13.5-ounce can coconut milk
2   cups water
3   teaspoons canola oil
1   cup onion, chopped
2   garlic cloves, minced
1   cup orange bell pepper, chopped
1   teaspoon salt
½   teaspoon black pepper
2   cups white rice *(the kind that cooks in about 20 minutes)*
2   cans black beans, drained and rinsed

COMBINE coconut milk and water in a bowl. In a medium stockpot over medium heat, heat oil, then sauté onion, garlic, bell pepper, salt and pepper until slightly tender. Add rice, coconut milk, water and beans. Cover, bring to a boil then reduce heat to low and cook 20 minutes. Serve with Jamaican Spiced Lamb. *(Serves 6)*

WINE: *Albarino, Pinot Gris, sparkling wine, or Viognier.*

Lamb and Artichoke Stew with Baked Rice

Artichoke is a thistle. Have you ever wondered who discovered we could eat some of these vegetables? We are lucky someone did.

¼ cup canola oil
2 pounds boneless lamb, cubed
3 cups onions, chopped
1 sweet yellow pepper, chopped
4 garlic cloves, crushed
½ cup fresh parsley, chopped
  salt and pepper to taste
6 ounces tomato paste
1 cup chicken stock
1 cup white wine, plus more if needed
1 14.5-ounce can of artichoke hearts, drained and halved
2 teaspoons dried dill
¼ teaspoon lemon zest

HEAT oil in 5 quart pot over high heat. Add lamb, and sear until lightly browned. Remove and set lamb aside, tented, in a bowl. Sauté onions, pepper, garlic and parsley. Add lamb back in plus any juices, salt, pepper, tomato paste, chicken stock and white wine. Simmer stew, covered, for 2½ hours.

MEANWHILE prepare rice. Preheat oven to 350°F.

Baked Rice

1 cup rice
2 tablespoons butter
½ cup chopped onion
½ teaspoon white pepper
2 cups chicken broth
½ cup red bell pepper, chopped
3 scallions, green only, chopped

RINSE rice with hot water. Melt butter in small saucepan and sauté onions for 5 minutes. Stir in rice, coating with butter, add white pepper and chicken broth and stir. Pour into covered casserole and bake 30 minutes. Remove from oven and stir in sweet peppers and green onion.

ADD artichokes, dill and lemon zest to stew. Add more wine if more liquid is needed. Simmer 15 more minutes or until tender. Serve lamb stew on baked rice. *(Serves 6)*

WINE: *We had a Bartlett's Mead, a dry white wine with honey aromas.*

Artichoke

Lamb and Morels
with Asparagus

This is a quick, delicious dish for two. Uncork a great bottle of wine,
relax and savor this simple meal.

¼ pound bacon
1 pound asparagus, woody ends cut off
3 cups Morel mushrooms, halved
3 tablespoons butter
  salt and pepper to taste
4 loin lamb chops, 1½-inches thick

FRY bacon, set aside to cool. When cooled, crumble bacon and reserve.

STEAM asparagus in a shallow pan with a little water, al dente. *(Cooked but still crisp)*

MELT butter in large skillet on medium heat. Add mushrooms, salt and pepper and cook for 5 minutes. Remove mushrooms from pan and set aside. Heat pan on high, add lamb chops and sear 3 minutes on each side for medium rare. Return mushrooms to pan and heat through, about 2 minutes.

PLACE lamb chops on warmed plate with Morel mushrooms on top, and asparagus on the side with bacon on top. *(Serves 2)*

WINE: *Rioja or Hermitage. We enjoyed a 1998 Rioja Grand Reserve, Fierra Cantabria.*

Lamb Chops with Saffron Orzo

4 1 ½-inch lamb rib chops
¾ teaspoon salt, divided
½ teaspoon black pepper, divided
3 tablespoons olive oil
2 garlic cloves, finely chopped
½ cup dry white wine
2 cups grape tomatoes, whole
1 teaspoon finely chopped fresh rosemary

PAT chops dry and sprinkle with ½ teaspoon salt and
¼ teaspoon pepper.

HEAT oil in large cast iron skillet over medium-high heat. Sear
lamb chops, turning over once, until golden and just cooked
through, 6 minutes total. Transfer lamb chops to a plate. Add garlic
to skillet and cook over medium heat for 30 seconds. Stir in wine,
tomatoes, rosemary, and remaining salt and pepper and simmer,
gently pressing on tomatoes until they collapse, about 10 minutes.
Keep warm while cooking orzo.

Saffron Orzo

1½ cups orzo
¼ teaspoon crumbled saffron threads
3 tablespoons unsalted butter
¼ cup finely grated Parmigiano-Reggiano cheese

COOK orzo with saffron in a 3-quart saucepan of boiling salted
water until al dente. Drain in colander and return to saucepan, then
stir in butter and cheese. Place lamb chops on warm plates with
orzo on the side and tomato-rosemary mixture spooned half on
and half off the lamb chop. Serve immediately. *(Serves 2 to 4)*

WINE: *young red Bordeaux or dry rose.*

Wicked Good Lamb Chops in a Balsamic Marinade with Baked Potato Wedges

⅓ cup balsamic vinegar
⅓ cup soy sauce
½ teaspoon Kate's Wicked Good Hot Sauce *(see recipe at right)*
1 tablespoon finely grated orange zest
8 two-inch lamb chops
salt and freshly ground pepper
½ cup blood orange oil *(or vegetable oil)*
½ cup red wine *(red Zinfandel)*
¼ cup balsamic vinegar

PREHEAT the oven to 450°F.

COMBINE in a large bowl vinegar, soy sauce, hot sauce and orange zest. Add lamb and marinate for 2 hours, turning once. Remove the lamb from the marinade and pat dry, reserve marinade. Season the lamb with salt and pepper. In a large skillet, heat oil until shimmering. Add the lamb and sear over moderately high heat until nicely browned, about 3 minutes on each side.

TRANSFER lamb to a rimmed baking sheet. Roast in the upper third of the oven for 15 minutes. Let the lamb rest for 10 minutes before serving on warmed plate.

ADD wine and vinegar to reserved marinade in skillet, reduce on medium-high heat for 5 minutes. Plate lamb and top with sauce alongside potato wedges.

Baked Potato Wedges

4 potatoes cut in wedge quarters
4 medium onions, quartered
¼ cup olive oil

> 1 teaspoon kosher salt
> ½ teaspoon coarsely ground pepper
> ½ teaspoon oregano
> 1 teaspoon thyme

PREHEAT oven to 375°F. Coat 9" x 13" shallow baking pan with cooking spray.

COMBINE potatoes and onions in pan. Drizzle oil over vegetables and sprinkle with salt, pepper, oregano, and thyme. Lightly stir vegetables to coat all sides with oil and seasonings; bake, uncovered, for 1 hour, or until fork-tender, turn occasionally to keep the vegetables from sticking to the bottom of the pan. Serve immediately. *(Serves 4)*

Kate's Wicked Good Hot Sauce

> 2 cup carrots, chopped
> 1 yellow onion, chopped
> 1½ cups apple cider vinegar
> ¼ cup lime juice
> 12 garlic cloves, chopped
> 1 teaspoon salt
> 1 tablespoon sugar
> 12 fresh Scotch Bonnet peppers, chopped

COMBINE all ingredients except peppers in saucepan. Boil 19 minutes or until carrots are soft. Add peppers, slightly cool and puree in blender until smooth.

POUR in sterilized jars and refrigerate.

WINE: *California or Oregon fruity Pinot Noir.*

COOK'S NOTE I follow regular canning instructions for a longer shelf life of this Hot Sauce.

Mustard Crumb Wrapped Lamb with Grilled Asparagus

We started our asparagus bed 5 years ago. It has been a labor of love. You have to wait another two years after planting to be able to even begin to harvest your first crop. And what a delicious crop it was that first year.

1	pound asparagus, ends cut off
3	tablespoons red apple balsamic vinegar*
2	tablespoons Meyer lemon juice
1	tablespoon olive oil
⅛	teaspoon black pepper

PREHEAT oven to 450°F. Preheat grill on high and spray grill racks with cooking spray.

COMBINE all ingredients in large zip closure bag; seal and marinate for 30 minutes while preparing lamb. Remove asparagus and discard marinade. Place asparagus on grill for 5 minutes on each side and serve aside lamb.

Mustard Crumb Wrapped Lamb

3	tablespoons unsalted butter
2	whole boneless lamb loins (about 1 pound each)
	salt and freshly ground pepper
¼	cup flour, for dredging
¼	cup plus 2 tablespoons Dijon mustard
1	cup coarse dry bread crumbs
2	tablespoons coarsely chopped flat-leaf parsley
2	teaspoons minced garlic
1	teaspoon minced shallot
2	teaspoons finely chopped oregano
2	teaspoons finely chopped basil
2	teaspoons freshly grated Parmesan cheese
5	tablespoons unsalted butter, melted

MELT butter in large ovenproof skillet. Season lamb with salt and pepper and dredge in flour. Add lamb to hot skillet and sear, turning once, about 6 minutes total. Cool lamb slightly, then pat dry and brush with mustard.

ON A PLATE combine bread crumbs with parsley, garlic, shallot, oregano, basil, Parmesan and melted butter. Roll lamb in crumb mixture, pressing it into the meat. Return lamb to the skillet and place in oven for about 10 minutes for medium-rare meat. Transfer to a work surface, cover loosely with foil and let stand for 5 minutes. Slice lamb in 1/3-inch thick pieces and serve. *(Serves 4)*

WINE: *chilled Beaujolais Village, almost dry Riesling or Ribeiro.*

*COOK'S NOTE red apple balsamic vinegar can be purchased at www.oldtownoil.com

Lamb Roast with Curry Sauce and Garam Masala Rice

Garam means "hot," and Masala means "spices." This spice mixture "heated" the body, according to ancient ayurvedic medicine. The blend of dry-roasted ground spices (which may contain up to 12 spices) changes per household depending on their tastes. It can include black pepper, cinnamon, cloves, coriander, cumin, cardamom, dried chili, fennel, ginger, mace and nutmeg. This is my favorite combination.

1	5 pound leg of lamb, bone in
2	garlic cloves, peeled and sliced
1	tablespoon fresh rosemary, slightly chopped
3	tablespoons olive oil
2	tablespoons red wine vinegar
1	teaspoon dried rosemary
1	teaspoon Worcestershire sauce
1	teaspoon sweet paprika
⅓	cup flour
½	teaspoon salt
1	tablespoon cane sugar
½	teaspoon ground black pepper

PREHEAT oven to 500°F with rack in middle of oven. Grease 9" x 13" roasting pan.

PIERCE lamb in several places and insert garlic slices and fresh rosemary.

COMBINE remaining ingredients to form a paste and rub all over meat to coat. Place lamb in roasting pan and immediately into preheated oven for 20 minutes to form a light crust. Reduce temperature to 325°F and bake lamb for 1 hour, or until internal temperature reaches 125°F for medium-rare.

Garam Masala Rice

2 tablespoons canola oil
1 medium sweet onion, halved and thinly sliced
1 teaspoon cumin, ground
½ teaspoon Mango Masala Seasoned Salt *(or sea salt)*
1 cup basmati rice
2 cups water
¾ teaspoon salt
2 teaspoons Garam Masala *(see recipe on next page)*
¾ cup frozen peas

HEAT oil over medium heat in small saucepan; sauté onions, cumin and Mango Masala Salt until onions are just tender. Add rice to pan with onions; add water and stir in salt and Garam Masala. Cover and bring to boil, reduce heat to low, keeping the rice covered at all times. After cooking 25 minutes, add peas and gently stir. Meanwhile begin sauce. Cook 10 minutes, or until water has evaporated and rice is tender.

Sauce

3 tablespoons butter
2 tablespoons flour
2 teaspoons curry powder
1 teaspoon sweet paprika
½ teaspoon dry mustard
1½ cups game or beef stock
¼ cup sherry
½ teaspoon salt

MELT butter in saucepan, add flour, curry, paprika and mustard; stir and cook for 2 minutes. Add stock and heat; stir until smooth and thick. Add sherry and salt, stir.

REMOVE lamb from oven and let rest, tented with aluminum foil for 10 minutes. Slice lamb, plate and spoon sauce over slices. Add rice on the side and serve immediately.

Garam Masala

1 tablespoon cardamom seeds
1 teaspoon whole cloves *(Penang*)*
1 teaspoon whole black peppercorns *(Tellicherry*)*
1 teaspoon whole black cumin seeds
2 inch stick cinnamon
⅓ of whole nutmeg
½ teaspoon coriander
½ teaspoon mace

COMBINE and grind in spice grinder, store in glass jar.

WINE: *Gigondas (France), Warwick Pinotage (South Africa).*

*COOK'S NOTE I really enjoy trying different varieties within the peppercorn family. I love them all, and they each have their place. Most spices can be purchased locally or through The Spice House (www.thespicehouse.com). I feel they have excellent quality spices.

*Whole Penang Cloves – native to southeast Asia, buds are picked before opening and taste and smell a little sweeter than others.

*Tellicherry Black Peppercorns – a variety of Malabar with an exquisite bold fruitiness.

Lamb-Stuffed Sweet Peppers

2   red bell peppers
2   yellow bell peppers
1   pound ground lamb
1   small yellow onion, chopped
¼   cup uncooked short grain brown rice
½   cup vegetable *(or beef)* stock
1   tablespoon tomato paste
½   teaspoon salt
1   teaspoon rosemary, chopped
¼   teaspoon lavender
¼   teaspoon thyme
¼   teaspoon white pepper
1   14 ½-ounce can stewed tomatoes, undrained
1   teaspoon oregano
1   tablespoon apple cider vinegar
½   teaspoon dried parsley

PREHEAT oven to 350°F. Grease covered 8" x 8" baking dish with non-stick cooking spray.

CUT tops off bell peppers; remove seeds and pith. Combine ground lamb, onion, rice, stock, paste and seasonings in large bowl, mixing lightly but thoroughly. Spoon into peppers; stand peppers in baking dish, stuffing side up.

COMBINE stewed tomatoes, oregano, vinegar, and parsley and pour over peppers. Cover dish and bake for 1½ hours, juices should show no pink color. (*Serves 4*)

WINE: *meaty Pinot Noir.*

Lamb with Blueberry Shallot Sauce and Glazed Carrots

1 3-pound boneless leg of lamb, rolled, tied, and trimmed of excess fat

¼ cup chopped shallots

2 tablespoons butter

1 tablespoon arrowroot *(or flour)*

1 tablespoon fresh thyme
(or ½ teaspoon dried thyme)

½ teaspoon fresh rosemary
(or ¼ teaspoon dried rosemary), crushed

½ cup dry red wine

½ cup water

1½ cups blueberries
rosemary sprigs for garnish *(optional)*

SAUTÉ shallots in butter on medium heat in saucepan. Add arrowroot, thyme and rosemary; cook and stir until mixture bubbles and thickens. Gradually add wine and water; stir in blueberries. Increase heat and stir until mixture thickens and boils; reduce heat and simmer 3 minutes.

SPRINKLE lamb with salt and pepper. Place lamb into a deep baking pan; pour 1 ½ cups Blueberry Shallot Sauce over lamb. Cover and refrigerate for 6 hours. Cover remaining sauce and refrigerate.

PREHEAT oven to 350°F.

REMOVE lamb from marinade and place on a rack in shallow baking pan; place in the lower half of the oven. Bake, uncovered, approximately 1 hour or until meat thermometer registers 125°F for medium rare, basting with marinade every 15 minutes.

Glazed Carrots

1½ tablespoons butter
1 pound carrots, sliced
½ cup chicken broth
2 teaspoons brown sugar
½ teaspoon salt
1 teaspoon thyme leaves, fresh
½ teaspoon lemon zest
½ teaspoon lemon juice

MELT butter in large sauce pan, on medium. Add carrots and stir to coat. Cook for 10 minutes. Add broth, brown sugar, salt, thyme and lemon zest; stir to coat. Cover and simmer until vegetables are just tender, 10 minutes. Uncover and increase heat, stirring frequently until liquid cooks down to a glaze. Stir in lemon juice and serve immediately.

REMOVE lamb from oven and transfer to cutting board; let stand 15 minutes before carving. Lamb will continue to cook; temperature may increase up to 10 degrees after removed from oven. Warm sauce, then divide lamb between 6 warmed plates; add glazed carrots and drizzle Blueberry Shallot Sauce over lamb. Garnish with fresh sprigs of rosemary. *(Serves 6)*

WINE: *red Burgundy or an off-dry Late Harvest Gewurzstraminer.*

Maine Maple Braised Lamb Chops with Ambercup Squash

Maine produces outstanding maple syrup, and Arnold Maple Sugar Farm House is a mind-boggling producer of this sweet elixir. It's past Jackman on your way to Quebec, 700 feet off Route 201 on the Hilton Cemetery Road in Sandy Bay Township. This manufacturing facility began producing maple syrup in the spring of 2000 from sap collected through 29,000 taps. They now have 5 pumping stations drawing sap from 45,000 taps over the 500 acres and carrying it underground to one manufacturing plant.

Owner Claude Rodrigue was gracious enough to take time out in the middle of his busy season to show me the operation. He and his son, Francoise, run, maintain, process and barrel the sap flowing from 5 miles of underground tubing into 55 gallon drums. The business goes 24/7 during maple sugar season, the two taking turns at napping, until the last maple sap is boiled.

One of the most interesting points I learned on this excursion was when the weather begins to turn warm outside it begins to turn the color of the maple syrup darker. This typically happens at the end of the season. It is also a more flavorful maple syrup and it is prized in commercial usage.

Ambercup Squash

1   ambercup squash, halved and deseeded
    (or butternut)
2   tablespoons Maine maple syrup
2   tablespoons butter
2   teaspoons kosher salt

PREHEAT oven to 375°F. Spray sided cookie sheet with cooking spray.

PLACE squash on cookie sheet face down and bake for 45 minutes or until tender. Cool, scrape out squash into bowl; add syrup, butter and salt, stir, cover and set aside.

Braised Lamb

8 lamb shoulder chops
1 tablespoon olive oil
½ cup apple cider
½ cup chicken broth
2 tablespoons Maine maple syrup
½ cup apple cider vinegar
1 McIntosh apple, peeled and sliced
8 dates, chopped
  salt and freshly ground pepper

HEAT oil in large skillet and sauté chops on high heat for 2 minutes each side.

COMBINE apple cider, broth, maple syrup and apple cider vinegar; add to lamb skillet. Simmer for 30 minutes or until lamb is tender. Remove lamb from pan, cover with foil to keep warm.

BRING skillet juices to boil, add apple and dates and cook until sauce has thickened, about 5 minutes. Return lamb to heat through, coating lamb with sauce. Add salt and pepper to taste.

ON WARMED PLATES serve lamb chops topped with sauce and squash on the side. (*Serves 6 to 8*)

WINE: *buttery Chardonnay or sparkling Shiraz.*

Marsala Morel Mushrooms over Grilled Lamb with Baked Potato Wedges

I first learned about Morel mushrooms when I went out to Oregon to help my girlfriend, Karen Kettlety, during lambing season on her farm. It was my first trip to Oregon and it won't be my last. I was captivated by the charm of the little town of Richmond and its surrounding landscapes. From the flat, green grassy fields to the hills, then mountains with snow on the peaks in the middle of May, all within 25 minutes.

It was spring! Lambing, morels, calving, cowboys and bee swarms. There were many unforgettable memories but the most vivid was seeing a beehive with two queens separate. First the hive split from the old fruit house where they were living; one queen stayed and the other took her crew and hung in the Quince bush out back while the scouts went to search for a new home. The next afternoon I was out, and there was this buzzing, a growing shadow, and all this energy. I looked up above the Black Walnut trees for the source and saw bees swarming together in an oval pattern, slowly moving away from the house. Very cool!

Back to the morel mushrooms! Morchella, the true morel, are these amazing cone head shape with a brain-like looking texture. The amazing flavor of these mushrooms will make this visual a delicacy in your mind and palate. If you can't find morels, try delicious oyster mushrooms instead.

Baked Potato Wedges

4	potatoes cut in wedge quarters
4	onions, quartered
¼	cup olive oil
1	teaspoon coarse (kosher) salt
½	teaspoon coarsely ground pepper
1	teaspoon dried rosemary
1	teaspoon dried thyme

PREHEAT oven to 375°F. Coat 9" x 13" shallow baking pan with cooking spray.

COMBINE potatoes and onions in pan. Drizzle oil over vegetables and sprinkle with salt, pepper, rosemary, and thyme. Lightly stir vegetables to coat all sides with oil and seasonings; bake, uncovered, for 1 hour, or until fork-tender, turn occasionally to keep the vegetables from sticking to the bottom of the pan. *(Meanwhile start lamb)*. Serve immediately.

Marsala Morel Mushrooms over Grilled Lamb

1	cup morel mushrooms *(or oyster mushrooms)*, halved
3	tablespoons olive oil
1	tablespoon fresh garlic, minced
3	tablespoons Marsala wine
1	teaspoon dried rosemary, ground
1	teaspoon salt
½	teaspoon pepper
½	teaspoon lavender
4	1½-inch loin lamb chops, salt and peppered

PREHEAT grill on high for lamb. Coat grill racks with cooking spray.

SAUTÉ mushrooms in olive oil and garlic for 3 minutes on medium-high. Add Marsala wine and cook another minute. Meanwhile grind rosemary, salt, pepper and lavender in grinder. Pat lamb dry and roll lamb in herbs to cover completely. Grill on high to your desired temperature; I prefer medium-rare for the best flavor. Place lamb on warmed plate with potato wedges and top with mushrooms. Serve immediately. *(Serves 4)*

WINE: *Cotes du Rhone or Mersault (white Burgundy).*

Mediterranean Lamb with Squash and Saffron Couscous

This is one the easiest lamb dishes with the most ingredients. It yeilds a multitude of textures, spices, and always results in an exceptional presentation. Kat grew her own butternut squash, and I honored this dish with it. Yum!

1	tablespoon olive oil
2	pounds boneless lamb shoulder, cubed or lamb stew meat
3	medium onions cut into eighths
6	cloves garlic, minced
2	tablespoons ground ginger
1	tablespoon ground cinnamon
½	teaspoon cayenne pepper
¼	teaspoon allspice
¼	teaspoon cloves, ground
1	14.5-ounce can diced tomatoes, undrained
1	cup water
1	15.5-ounce can chickpeas, drained
1	cup chopped dates
½	teaspoon salt
1	small butternut squash, peeled, seeded and cut into 1-inch pieces
2	cups chicken stock
1½	cups water
¼	teaspoon salt
¼	teaspoon saffron threads, crushed
1½	cups couscous
⅓	cup chopped fresh cilantro

HEAT oil in large stockpot over medium heat; add lamb, stirring occasionally, for 10 minutes until browned. Add onions, garlic, ginger, cinnamon, cayenne, allspice and cloves; stir 1 minute. Add tomatoes and water. Bring to a boil and reduce heat. Cover and simmer 1 hour.

REMOVE 1 cup liquid from lamb mixture and discard. Continue simmering lamb, covered, another 30 minutes. Add chickpeas, dates and salt; simmer 20 minutes or until lamb is tender. Uncover and simmer until liquid is slightly thickened and reduced by half.

ADD butternut squash to chicken stock in a medium saucepan. Cover and bring to a boil over high heat. Lower heat and simmer, stirring frequently, about 20 minutes or until squash is tender. Meanwhile, prepare couscous.

COMBINE water, salt and saffron in medium saucepan. Bring to boil and stir in couscous. Cover; remove from heat. Let stand 5 minutes or until liquid is absorbed.

PLACE couscous on a warmed serving platter. Form well in middle and spoon in lamb stew; top with squash and sprinkle with cilantro. *(Serves 6 to 8)*

WINE: *white Chateaunauf du Pape.*

Mediterranean Lamb, Sausage and Orange Slices with Mushroom Pilaf

6 rosemary branches
1½ pounds chunked lamb from shoulder
½ pound sweet sausage links
3 navel oranges

PREHEAT oven to 450°F. Coat 9" x 13" roasting pan with cooking spray.

LAY rosemary branches on the bottom of roasting pan and top them with sausage; prick the sausage in a few places with a thin-bladed knife. Put in oven for 15 minutes, turning once or twice to remove some juices and until browned. Remove sausage from pan and set aside. Prepare pilaf.

Mushroom Pilaf

2 tablespoons butter
2 tablespoons lemon olive oil
1 onion, finely chopped
2 garlic cloves, crushed
2 cups long-grain rice, washed, soaked in cold water for 30 minutes and drained
4 ounces button mushrooms, clean and sliced
1 teaspoon salt
½ teaspoon black pepper
4 cups hot chicken stock
1 bay leaf
⅛ teaspoon lemon zest
1 tablespoon unsalted butter
2 tablespoons raisins
10 kalamata olives, slightly chopped

COMBINE butter and oil in sauce pan on medium high heat. Add onion and garlic, sauté 5 minutes. Add rice, stirring constantly for 5 minutes. Add mushrooms, salt and pepper, stirring constantly for 4 minutes. Add stock, bay leaf and lemon zest; bring to a boil. Reduce heat, cover and simmer for 20 minutes or until liquid is absorbed.

MEANWHILE peel oranges and cut them into ¼-inch thick slices. Layer lamb on rosemary branches, then sausage and orange slices; bake covered for 20 minutes. Remove cover and bake until the sausage is cooked through, about 5 more minutes.

FINISH pilaf by melting butter in small frying-pan, add raisins and fry until raisins are puffed up. Remove bay leaf from pilaf. Plate mushroom pilaf on warmed plates and scatter raisins and olives over the top. Serve with lamb and sausage chunks, discarding rosemary stems and oranges. (*Serves 4*)

WINE: *We liked Dragonfly Winey's Blueberry Bliss.*

Mexican Lamb Chili

You will see many smaller recipes embedded within larger recipes, like my homeade chili pepper. There are several purveyors that have great spice combinations, however, I just like to grind my own. Try it sometime and see if you can taste the difference.

¼ cup canola oil
8 cloves garlic
1 large onion, diced
2 pounds lamb stew meat, in small chunks
2 tablespoons chili powder *(see recipe at right)*
1 tablespoon Mexican oregano
1 tablespoon ground coriander
3 cups chicken stock
2 16-ounce cans diced tomatoes
1 16-ounce jar roasted yellow peppers, drained, rinsed and chopped
3 tablespoons tomato paste
1 tablespoon Worcestershire sauce
2 cans black beans, drained
salt and freshly ground black pepper to taste
¼ cup chopped cilantro
¼ cup sour cream, garnish optional

HEAT oil in a large saucepan over high heat; add garlic and onion and stir for 2 minutes. Add lamb, chili powder, oregano and coriander. Cook for 5 minutes. Add stock, tomatoes, peppers, paste and Worcestershire sauce. Simmer, stirring occasionally, for 30 minutes. Add beans, salt and pepper. Simmer another 30 minutes.

SPRINKLE chili with cilantro and top with a dollop of sour cream. Serve with a crusty bread. *(Serves 6)*

My Spicy Chili Powder

3 tablespoons sweet Ancho chili pepper
3 tablespoons cayenne chili powder
1 tablespoon crushed red peppers
1 tablespoon roasted ground cumin
1½ tablespoons dried garlic powder
1½ tablespoons Mexican oregano

GRIND all ingredients together in spice or coffee grinder; store in glass jar.

WINE: *Barbera, Chilean Cabernet Sauvignon, Gruner Veltliner or a cold Shipyard Fuggles IPA beer.*

Mexican Lamb Roast with Vegetable Rice

Lamb shoulders work well slow-roasting. It is a very forgiving cut, with plenty of lubricating fat; long cooking at low heat makes this roast very succulent and tender.

My tester Devorah Rifka says "I would emphasize that dry roasting and grinding of the spices really makes a difference, and they are worth it!"

1	5 pound lamb shoulder *(or leg)* roast*
2	teaspoons cumin seeds
3	tablespoons whole black peppercorns
3	tablespoons dried oregano
3	tablespoons dried thyme leaves
1	teaspoon sea salt
3	dried chipotle chilies, chopped, divided
3	tablespoons olive oil
1	cup red wine *(Cabernet Sauvignon)*
3	cups beef stock
	salt and pepper to taste

PREHEAT oven to 275°F. Grease shallow roasting pan. Place rack on lowest rung in oven.

SAUTÉ cumin seeds, peppercorns, oregano, and thyme over medium heat in dry cast-iron skillet to release flavors. Stir frequently and remove when they start to smoke. Add salt and one chopped chipotle chili. Cool and grind the spices into a fine powder. Reserve other chopped chipotles for much later.

RUB lamb with olive oil and spice mixture. Place lamb in a shallow roasting pan. Roast for 8 hours. *(One hour before lamb is done prepare the rice – see recipe at right)*. When finished cooking, lift lamb from roasting pan and place on warm dish, tented with aluminum foil. Let it rest for 20 minutes to keep all the juices in the lamb.

PLACE roasting pan on stove on medium heat, add wine and scrape any bits off the bottom. Reduce for 5 minutes. Pour into small pan, add stock and reserved chipotles. Reduce over high heat, stirring occasionally, until reduced by two-thirds. Carve lamb and serve on platter with rice medley; spoon sauce over lamb.

Vegetable Rice

2	teaspoons canola oil
1	cup brown rice
½	cup chopped onion
1½	cups carrots, finely diced
1	garlic clove, crushed
1½	cups stewed tomatoes, pureed
1	cup chicken broth
1	teaspoon oregano
½	teaspoon salt
½	cup frozen green peas
2	tablespoons minced fresh flat-leaf parsley

HEAT oil over medium heat in saucepan; add rice and onion and stir for 10 minutes until golden brown. Add carrots and garlic and cook one more minute. Add tomatoes, broth, oregano and salt; stir and bring to a boil. Reduce heat and simmer, covered, for 35 minutes or until liquid is absorbed. Remove from heat; stir in peas. Let stand for 10 minutes, covered. Serve alongside lamb.

WINE: *Chenin Blanc, red Zinfandel, or Valpolicella.*

***COOK'S NOTE** If you substitute a leg roast for a shoulder roast, reduce cooking time by 2 hours.

Mongolian Lamb and Noodle Salad

I recently had a hot entrée served with a cold side dish at a restaurant and remembered how refreshing the combination can be. It made me take notice of the texture of the cold, thinly sliced pea pods with such a light dressing.

2½	pound lamb shoulder or leg, sliced across grain into thin strips*
2	tablespoons dark soy sauce
2	tablespoons red wine vinegar
2	tablespoons chicken stock
1	teaspoon brown sugar
1	teaspoon sesame oil
3	tablespoons peanut oil
5	garlic cloves, minced
1	teaspoon chili paste
6	scallions, cut into 1-inch lengths
½	teaspoon salt

COMBINE soy, vinegar, stock, sugar, and sesame oil. Marinate the lamb for 1 hour.

PREHEAT wok or large non-stick fry pan on medium-high to high heat, and add peanut oil. When oil is hot, add garlic and chili paste. Stir-fry for 30 seconds, and add the lamb without the marinade. Let the lamb sear until it loses its pinkness *(about 2 minutes)*. Add scallions and salt. Stir-fry for another minute. Serve with noodle salad.

Dressing

½ cup seasoned rice vinegar
2 tablespoons olive oil
1 teaspoon sesame oil
3 cloves of garlic, minced
2 teaspoons soy sauce
2 teaspoons sugar

COMBINE all ingredients; let sit for 1 hour before tossing with noodles.

Noodle Salad

½ cup cilantro leaves, chopped
2 green onions, finely diced
½ red bell pepper, thinly sliced
½ yellow bell pepper, thinly sliced
1 cup shredded carrots
½ cup toasted peanuts
½ pound soba noodles, cooked per instructions

COMBINE all prepared ingredients and toss with dressing.
(Serves 8)

WINE: *Spanish Albarino or a Sapporo Beer.*

*COOK'S NOTE lamb slices more easily if slightly frozen.

Moroccan Spiced Lamb with Balsamic Vinaigrette Salad

It was one of those beautiful Saturday's that Maine is known for; bright cloudless blue skies, light breeze and no black flies! Don and I had been out early doing yard work, noon came around and we were starved. I headed to the fridge to see what I had to work with to make lunch: lamb stew meat, salad fixings and cupboards full of spices. As I was rummaging through I was thinking about this dish I had in Agidir, North Africa. I came up with this combination of spices.

Don fired up the grill and then matched the spice mixture with a chilled red Zinfandel and we settled into our lounge chairs. The combination of spices, textures and the chilled wine was so wonderful that we finished the bottle, never finished our yard work and really enjoyed when Dave and Joan stopped by for a visit. This was a perfect Saturday on MDI.

½	teaspoon ground roasted cumin
¼	teaspoon ground cardamom
¼	teaspoon ground allspice
¼	teaspoon freshly ground pepper
¼	teaspoon ground ginger
¼	teaspoon cayenne pepper
¼	teaspoon cinnamon
1½	teaspoons kosher salt
3	garlic cloves, minced
4	1-inch lamb loin chops
2	tablespoons vegetable oil
1	tablespoon chopped cilantro
4	cups mixed greens
¼	cup red onion, sliced very thin
½	cup goat cheese, crumbled
	balsamic vinaigrette *(see recipe at right)*

MIX dry spices in a small bowl with salt. Pat garlic all over the lamb chops and sprinkle with the spice mixture.

HEAT the vegetable oil in a large cast iron skillet. Add the chops and cook over moderately high heat, turning once, for about 6 minutes for medium-rare. Divide the chops between four plates, garnish with the cilantro and serve with greens and red onion topped with goat cheese and balsamic vinaigrette.

Balsamic Vinaigrette

- ½ cup extra-virgin olive oil
- 3 tablespoons balsamic vinegar
- ½ teaspoon dried thyme leaves
- ½ teaspoon dried oregano leaves
- ½ teaspoon freshly ground black pepper

PLACE vinegar in a bowl and whisk in olive oil in a slow stream to combine. Add seasonings and pepper and whisk to distribute herbs and spice throughout the dressing. *(Serves 4)*

WINE: *medium, spicy Zinfandel. We loved the Brown Vineyard Chiles Valley Zinfandel, chilled.*

Moussaka

*You may hear me say this a lot, and you'll know I mean it: try Meyer lemons!
You can cut them in half and eat them as is; they are so sweet! I use them
whenever I can or just as a snack, although I do take the zest and dry it for all
those moments when I just need a little something! Thanks Deke for the
continued supply of Meyer Lemons off your Meyer Lemon tree
from your backyard, in San Francisco.*

2	cups tomatoes, halved
2	large eggplants
	kosher salt and freshly ground black pepper
	extra-virgin olive oil
1	medium onion, chopped
4	garlic cloves, minced
½	Meyer lemon, sliced in thin circles
¼	cup fresh oregano leaves, chopped
¾	cup fresh flat-leaf parsley, chopped
1½	pounds ground lamb
½	teaspoon freshly ground cinnamon
1	cup goat feta cheese, crumbled *(or regular feta)*
½	cup freshly grated Parmesan
½	cup fresh bread crumbs

PREHEAT oven to 350°F. Spray four sided baking sheet and 9" x 12"
baking dish. Place tomatoes on baking sheet, skin side down. Bake
for 30 minutes.

CUT off eggplant stems, peel and cut lengthwise into ½-inch thick
slices. Season all the pieces of eggplant with salt and pepper on
both sides. Coat a large non-stick skillet with oil and heat over
medium heat. Fry the eggplant in batches in a single layer,
browning on both sides, adding more oil as necessary. Drain
eggplant after frying on paper towels.

ADD more oil to skillet; add onion, garlic, lemon slices, oregano, and parsley. Cook and stir until soft and fragrant, about 3 minutes. Add ground lamb and cinnamon. Stir in roasted tomatoes and simmer until liquid has evaporated. Remove from heat.

LINE sprayed baking dish with ½ of the eggplant slices, completely covering the bottom. Spread meat sauce over eggplant, even out with spatula. Sprinkle with cheeses, add top layer of eggplant. Cover top with even layer of bread crumbs. Spray crumbs with non-stick vegetable spray. Bake for 30 minutes, covered; remove cover and bake 10 more minutes or until top is golden. Let cool 10 minutes before serving. (*Serves 4*)

WINE: *Hermitage.*

Deke's Meyer Lemon tree

Mustard-Crusted Lamb Salad with Blue Cheese and Fig Balsamic Vinaigrette

4   cups baby spinach, cleaned and dried
1   thin slice red onion
1   small tomato, sliced
½   cup crumbled blue cheese
2   tablespoons Dijon mustard
8   ounces lamb tenderloin, cut across the grain
    into thin slices
    fig balsamic vinaigrette *(see recipe below)*

ARRANGE spinach, onions and tomato on two dinner plates; sprinkle cheese on top. Set aside.

SPREAD a thin layer of mustard over both sides of lamb slices. Heat a small, non-stick skillet over medium-high heat and cook lamb slices, about 1 minute per side or until browned. Place lamb slices on top of spinach. Drizzle vinaigrette over salad. *(Serves 2)*

Fig Balsamic Vinaigrette

2   tablespoons fig balsamic vinegar*
1   tablespoon red wine vinegar
1   tablespoon Dijon mustard
1   teaspoon light brown sugar
2   garlic cloves, minced
½   teaspoon salt
¼   teaspoon freshly ground black pepper
¾   cup extra virgin olive oil

WHISK all ingredients except the oil, in a bowl, until mixed. Gradually whisk in the oil until smooth. *(Yields about 1 cup)*

WINE: Joseph Drouhin Beaujolais-Villages (chilled) or Montinore (Oregon) Almost Dry Riesling.

*COOK'S NOTE fig balsamic vinegar is available wherever specialty olive oils and vinegars are sold, including LeRoux Kitchen in Portland Maine (www.lerouxkitchen.com) and Old Town Oil in Chicago (www.oldtownoil.com).

Blue Cheese

Parmesan Kalamata Encrusted Lamb with Braised Cremini Mushrooms

The second time I visited Greece was when my brother Mark, sister-in-law Angie and nephew Nicholas were living there in 1986. Mark was serving in the US Air Force, stationed in Athens, and loving the Greek culture. His second son, Jeramey, was born there. We took a 5 day trip around the Peloponnese where Kalamata is, in southern Greece. Kalamata is most well-known to us for their succulent dark olives. And Kalamata is renowned as the land of the Kalamatianos dance and the silk kerchief, honey-eyed figs and the honey-covered sesame sweet called pasteli (which is so delicious!).

12	1-inch lamb loin chops
¾	cup Parmesan cheese, grated
1	tablespoon garlic, minced
¾	cup kalamata olives, finely chopped
1	tablespoon fresh thyme, chopped
½	teaspoon dried Greek oregano *(or regular oregano)*
3	tablespoons olive oil
¼	cup lemon olive oil *(or olive oil &* *¼ teaspoon lemon zest)*

PREHEAT oven to 400°F. Spray 9" x 13" baking pan with non-stick vegetable spray.

COMBINE Parmesan cheese, garlic, kalamata olives, thyme, Greek oregano and olive oil. Spread 1 tablespoon of cheese mixture evenly on one side of each chop. Set aside. Meanwhile prepare mushrooms.

Braised Cremini Mushrooms

12 ounces cremini or button mushrooms, sliced thin
¼ cup red wine
1 teaspoon fresh garlic, minced
1 teaspoon dried marjoram
½ teaspoon dried thyme
¼ teaspoon Vulcan Fire Salt*
   (or equal parts of sea salt and red pepper flakes)

COMBINE mushrooms, red wine, garlic, marjoram, thyme, Vulcan Salt in saucepan; cover and cook on medium for 5 minutes. Remove lid and cook until liquid completely reduced. Finish chops.

PREHEAT lemon olive oil for lamb in cast-iron skillet. Place chops in skillet with cheese mixture side up. Brown chops; 1 minute per side. Place chops on baking pan and into oven for 6 minutes or until the chops reach an internal temperature of 140°F for medium. (*Serves 4 to 6*)

WINE: *Conde de Valdemar Rioja Crianza, Spain or Prunotto Barbera D'Asti Fuilot, Italy.*

*COOK'S NOTE Vulcan Fire Salt—I met the man who created this wonderful, firey salt. It was named in honor of the Roman god of fire, Vulcan. It is also great on popcorn, pizza, and delicious in Bloody Mary's. (www.thespicehouse.com)

Pomegranate Lamb, Chestnuts and Apricots over Saffron Rice

The second time testing this recipe I found the chestnuts in the pantry and decided to throw them in on a whim to make the dish a little thicker. It really added to the color contrast, texture and flavor.

3	tablespoons olive oil
3	cups onions, chopped
5	garlic cloves, chopped
1½	pounds boneless lamb, cut in ½" cubes
½	teaspoon turmeric, ground
1	teaspoon salt
½	teaspoon black pepper
¼	teaspoon saffron threads, crushed
½	teaspoon cinnamon, ground
1	cup walnuts, minced
¾	cup dried apricots*, chopped
2	tablespoons tomato paste
2	cups chicken stock
2	tablespoons pomegranate molasses*
	(or 1 cup pomegranate juice reduced to 2 tablespoons)
3	tablespoons lime juice freshly squeezed
1½	cup chestnuts, chopped fine
1	teaspoon apricot preserves
4	tablespoons fresh mint as garnish

HEAT oil in a heavy casserole over medium heat; add onions and garlic and sauté for 5 minutes. Raise heat to high, add lamb, turmeric, salt and pepper, and brown meat on all sides. Stir in saffron, cinnamon, walnuts, apricots, tomato paste, chicken stock and pomegranate molasses. Bring to a boil, reduce heat, cover and simmer for 1½ hours.

ADD lime juice, chestnuts and apricot preserves; stir, cover and simmer for 15 more minutes. Serve over bed of saffron rice.

Saffron Rice

- 2 cups basmati rice
- 1 teaspoon saffron threads
- 4 cups boiling water, divided
- 3 tablespoons butter
- 1 2-inch stick of cinnamon
- 5 whole cloves
- 1 teaspoon salt
- ½ teaspoon ground cardamom

PLACE saffron threads in small bowl and cover with 3 tablespoons of boiling water. Soak for 10 minutes.

HEAT butter over medium heat in stockpot. Add cinnamon and cloves and stir well. Add rice and stir for about 5 minutes. Pour in 4 cups of boiling water, salt, and the cardamom. Bring to boil over high heat. Add saffron and soaking water; stir gently. Cover, reduce heat, and cook for 20 minutes. Fluff and serve. (*Serves 6*)

WINE: *Pinot Noir or red Zinfandel.*

*COOK'S NOTE great jumbo dried apricots from Sweet Energy (*see Resources*). Pomegranate molasses is available from The Spice House (*see Resources*) and other specialty food stores.

Porcini Encrusted Lamb Chops with Sweet Pepper and Asparagus Rice Salad

¾ cup butter, room temperature
3 tablespoons fresh chives, chopped
1½ tablespoons fresh tarragon, chopped
1 small garlic clove, pressed
¼ teaspoon salt
6 1¼-inch loin lamb chops
  salt and pepper to taste
¼ cup porcini mushroom powder*

MIX first 5 ingredients together in small bowl to make herb butter. Sprinkle chops with salt and pepper. Press porcini powder into chops to coat both sides well.

MELT 2 tablespoons herb butter in heavy large nonstick skillet over medium heat. Add chops to skillet and cook to desired doneness, about 5 minutes per side for medium-rare. Transfer chops to plates. Spoon rounded tablespoon of herb butter atop each chop and serve with rice salad (*see below*).

Tahini Dressing

1 garlic clove, chopped
¼ cup tahini
  zest of one lemon
3 tablespoons freshly squeezed lemon juice
¼ cup extra-virgin olive oil
2 tablespoons hot water
½ teaspoon sea salt

WHISK garlic, tahini, lemon zest, juice, and olive oil. Add hot water to thin and then salt. Set aside.

Asparagus Rice Salad

3   tablespoons extra-virgin olive oil
1   16-ounce can of chickpeas, drained
½   teaspoon sea salt, divided
2   cloves garlic, minced
1   onion, chopped
1   bunch asparagus cut in 1-inch segments
3   cups brown rice, cooked
1   cup red bell pepper, chopped
    almond slivers for garnish *(optional)*

HEAT olive oil in big skillet over medium-high heat. Add chickpeas and ¼ teaspoon sea salt and sauté for 2 minutes. Add garlic and onions; stir 1 minute. Add asparagus and ¼ teaspoon sea salt, cover with a lid and steam for 3 minutes or until asparagus brightens and softens a bit. Uncover and stir in cooked rice and pepper. Serve tossed with half the Tahini Dressing and more dressing on the side for individual tastes. Plate with lamb and top with almond slivers. (*Serves 4 to 6*)

WINE: *Cotes du Rhone (Terre du Mistral). We had a 2006 Stanley Lambert Three's Company that went well. It has 25% Granche, 28% Malbec, and 15% Merlot. DaVine Wines in Bowdoinham carrys the Stanley Lambert from Barossa Valley, Australia.*

*COOK'S NOTE Porcini Mushroom Powder available at Maine Goodies, www.mainegoodies.com.

Roast Lamb Shoulder Provencal with Anise Carrots

The wine with the meal can add so much to the experience. We drank a decanted 1998 Beaucastel Chateauneuf du Pape with this recipe. I loved the chewiness and the long finish. It just kept opening all night. The Wine Spectator described it as "very youthful, with a juicy blast of red plum and fig fruit flavors on a racy frame, this also has plenty of spice, tar, plum cake and mineral in reserve, as the finish shows more structure and slowly darkens with time in the glass." And then it is only just starting to hit its stride!

1	3 to 4-pound butterflied lamb shoulder*
¼	cup extra virgin olive oil
2	teaspoons garlic, minced
1	teaspoon fennel seeds
1	tablespoon fresh lavender leaves (*or 1 teaspoon dried*)
1	tablespoon fresh rosemary leaves (*or 1 teaspoon dried*)
2	teaspoons fresh thyme leaves
	salt and black pepper to taste
	lavender flowers or rosemary sprigs for garnish (*if available*)
	lemon wedges for serving

PREHEAT the broiler, placing the rack at least 4 inches from the heat source.

TRIM the lamb of any excess fat and, if any parts seem overly thick, make a horizontal cut in the meat so they lie fairly flat.

COMBINE the oil, garlic, fennel seeds, and herbs with some salt and pepper. Use a thin-bladed knife to poke some holes in the lamb and stick a little bit of the mixture into each of them; rub the meat with remaining mixture.

BROIL the meat until it is nicely browned, even a little charred, on both sides, 25 to 30 minutes, and the internal temperature at the thickest part is about 125°F; this will give you some lamb that is quite rare as well as some that is nearly well done. Let rest for 5 minutes before slicing thinly. Garnish the lamb with rosemary or lavender and serve with lemon wedges and Anise Carrots.

Anise Carrots

1 pound of carrots, cut julienne*
1 star of anise
2 cups water
salt and butter *(optional)*

PLACE carrots in top of steamer, and water and anise star in bottom pot. Steam the carrots for 20 minutes. Salt, butter and enjoy! (*Serves 6*)

> **WINE:** *Chateauneuf du Pape, or a Bandol from Provence (Domaine Tempier).*

***COOK'S NOTE** If you grill the boneless lamb shoulder, grill over lower heat because it is higher in fat and this will prevent burning. A julienne carrot is cut in 3-inch lengths and then in matchstick widths.

Roasted Spicy Bordeaux Lamb Leg with Sweet Onion and Cheddar Bake

My testers (Sandy, Jack and crew) had a celebration gathering over this recipe. They prepared, tested, marinated, roasted, combined, ate and just had a grand time. Sandy enjoys cooking as much as I do and her detailed feedback is always invaluable and a pleasure to read. She recommended adding broccoli rabe on the plate for color. Presentation is a very important part of the meal; entice the eyes and fill the belly with satisfaction.

1	5-pound leg of lamb, de-boned and tied
1	cup red Bordeaux style wine
2	tablespoons concentrated orange juice
¼	cup water
½	cup shallots, minced
2	tablespoons vegetable oil
¼	cup chili powder
1	tablespoon brown sugar
1	teaspoon cumin, roasted and ground
1	teaspoon dried leaf oregano, crumbled
½	teaspoon salt
½	teaspoon ground black pepper

COMBINE all ingredients, except lamb, in a bowl. Place the lamb in a deep stainless steel or glass dish. Pour marinade over lamb and turn to coat well. Cover and refrigerate overnight, turning occasionally.

PREHEAT oven to 450°F. Drain lamb, reserve marinade; place on roasting rack in pan. Roast for 15 minutes. Reduce temperature to 325°F and pour marinade over lamb; baste frequently, for 1-1½ hours, or until done, about 125°F for medium-rare. Add a little boiling water to prevent juices from cooking down and burning. Let roast stand for 10 minutes. Carve and serve with skimmed pan juices.

Sweet Onion and Cheddar Bake

6 cups sweet onions, peeled and thinly sliced
2 teaspoons kosher salt
¼ cup butter
¼ cup flour
1 teaspoon salt
¼ teaspoon white pepper
1½ cups milk
1 cup cheddar, shredded
½ cup bread crumbs tossed with 1 tablespoon melted butter

COOK onions in boiling salted water for 15 minutes. Drain and transfer to buttered 9" x 9" baking dish.

PREHEAT second oven to 350°F.

MELT butter in saucepan on low heat; stir in flour, salt and white pepper. Add milk, stirring constantly, and cook until smooth and thickened. Add cheese and stir until cheese is melted and blended. Pour sauce over onions and top with buttered bread crumbs. Bake for 25 minutes uncovered, or until thoroughly heated and lightly browned. (*Serves 6 to 8*)

WINE: *Syrah (Goose Ridge) or Tempranillo from Ribera del Duero - tighter and drier than a Rioja.*

COOK'S NOTE If you do not have two ovens, prepare onion dish first and heat through when lamb roast is resting.

TESTER'S NOTE Sandy's crew enjoyed Jacks' (Scott/Sawyer's Specialty) pick of wines. They chose a 2003 Goose Ridge Syrah; second a 2005 Peltier Station Petite Syrah; and finally a 2005 St. Francis Old Vine Zin. They concluded that the Syrah went the best.

Rosemary Lamb Roast with Portabella Sauce and Goat Cheese Polenta

1   3 - 4 pound lamb shoulder
3   teaspoons crushed dried rosemary, divided
1   teaspoon coarse kosher salt
1   teaspoon freshly ground Tellicherry black pepper
¼   cup plus 1 tablespoon olive oil, divided
1   cup boiling water
1   ounce dried porcini mushrooms
2   tablespoons butter, room temperature, divided
6   ounces fresh portabella mushrooms
    cut into ¼ inch thick slices
2   garlic cloves, minced
1   tablespoon all-purpose flour
¾   cup lamb broth *(or beef stock)*
½   cup dry red wine
1   bunch fresh rosemary *(for garnish)*

PLACE roast, fat side up, in heavy roasting pan. Mix 2 teaspoons crushed rosemary, salt and pepper in small bowl. Stir in ¼ cup oil. Rub mixture all over roast. Cover and chill all day. Let stand at room temperature 45 minutes before roasting.

COMBINE boiling water and porcinis; let soak until mushrooms soften, about 30 minutes. Strain soaking liquid through fine strainer set over measuring cup; reserve liquid. If needed, add enough water to soaking liquid to measure 1 cup. Coarsely chop porcinis.

MELT 1 tablespoon butter with remaining 1 tablespoon oil in large skillet over medium-high heat. Add fresh mushrooms; sauté until browned, about 6 minutes. Add porcini and garlic; stir 1 minute.

Remove from heat. Combine flour, remaining 1 tablespoon butter, and remaining crushed rosemary in small bowl; mash with fork to smooth paste. *(Porcini soaking liquid, mushroom mixture and flour-butter mixture can be made 1 day ahead)*. Cover separately; chill.

PREHEAT oven to 350°F.

PLACE lamb in bottom third of oven. Cook roast until instant-read thermometer inserted straight down into top center of roast registers 125°F to 130°F for medium-rare, about 1 hour.

Meanwhile, start Goat Cheese Polenta *(see below)*. Transfer roast to platter; cover loosely with foil and rest 15 minutes. Skim any fat from top of pan juices *(there will be a small amount of pan drippings)*; reserve juices in pan.

Goat Cheese Polenta

- 2 tablespoons butter
- 2 sprigs fresh thyme
- 1 bay leaf
- 5 cups chicken stock

1 cup medium-course cornmeal
¼ cup fresh goat cheese
1 teaspoon salt
¼ teaspoon white pepper

COMBINE butter, thyme, bay leaf, and chicken stock in 4 quart saucepan over medium heat. Bring to boil, and gradually add cornmeal, whisking constantly to avoid lumps. Lower heat and continue to cook the polenta uncovered until the mixture thickens, about 45 minutes. *(Make sauce, below, before polenta is done)*. Once the polenta is thick, remove it from the heat and whisk in goat cheese, salt and white pepper. Serve immediately.

TO MAKE SAUCE set roasting pan atop burners over medium-high heat. Add 1 cup reserved porcini soaking liquid, broth, and wine; bring to boil, scraping up any browned bits. Add mushroom mixture, then flour-butter mixture; whisk constantly over medium-high heat until sauce thickens, about 2 minutes. Season with salt and pepper and serve with polenta and steamed carrots. *(Serves 6 to 8)*

WINE: *Cabernet Sauvignon, Rose Champagne, Shiraz or red Zinfandel.*

Spicy Island Lamb

2	pounds lamb stew meat
1	lime, juiced
1	tablespoon salt
1	teaspoon freshly ground black pepper
1	Scotch Bonnet Pepper, seeded and minced
½	teaspoon dried thyme
½	teaspoon ground allspice *(dry pimento berries)*
3	tablespoons curry powder
2	whole scallions, sliced
1	onion, sliced
3	cloves garlic, minced
¼	cup garlic olive oil
3	large tomatoes, diced
½	cup coconut milk
5	cups water

RUB lime juice over lamb, place in a bowl, then add salt, black pepper, Scotch Bonnet, thyme, allspice, curry powder, scallions, onion and garlic. Marinate for 5 hours in the refrigerator.

HEAT oil in a skillet until it is very hot and sauté the lamb until golden brown. Then add the marinade, tomatoes and coconut milk, and simmer for approximately 3 more minutes. Add water, reduce heat and simmer, covered, for 2 hours stirring occasionally until meat is tender. Serve with a flat bread and sour cream *(in case the heat gets you!)*. *(Serves 4)*

WINE: *Red Stripe Beer, Alsatian, Riesling, Pinot Noir. We've tested this recipe with Elk Cove Willamette Valley Pinot Noir (Oregon) and Chateau Ste. Michelle Eroica Riesling.*

Spanish Lamb with an Apricot Glaze, Couscous and Asiago Carrot Patties

1	tablespoon dried rosemary
1	teaspoon garlic salt
1	teaspoon dried marjoram
1	teaspoon black pepper
1	teaspoon salt
2	tablespoons olive oil
12	rib lamb chops, 1¼-inch thick
3	tablespoons canola oil
1	tablespoon unsalted butter
½	cup sweet onions, chopped
1	cup dry sherry
⅓	cup dried apricots, finely chopped
3	tablespoons brown sugar
1	tablespoon fresh parsley, chopped
2	cups chicken stock
1	cup couscous

COMBINE rosemary, garlic salt, marjoram, black pepper and salt for rub in spice grinder, pulse to combine well. Transfer to bowl and whisk in olive oil. Rub liberally over both sides of lamb chops. Marinate for 30 minutes at room temperature. Start carrot patties.

Carrot Patties

1½	cups carrots, cooked and mashed
1	cup potatoes, cooked and mashed
2	tablespoons butter, melted
¼	cup grated Asiago cheese
¼	cup chopped parsley, chopped fresh

    2   tablespoons dry breadcrumbs
    1   egg yolk
    ½   teaspoon salt
    ¼   teaspoon white pepper
    ⅛   teaspoon cayenne pepper
        flour
        canola oil

COMBINE all ingredients, except flour and oil. Shape into 8 carrot patties and dust each lightly with flour. Fry in hot oil until browned on both sides; drain on paper towels.

BRING chicken stock to boil, add couscous, cover and cook 5 minutes.

HEAT canola oil in cast-iron skillet on high heat, add lamb chops and sear on both sides, about 2 minutes per side for medium rare. Remove chops onto warmed plate with aluminum tent. Discard any fat from skillet.

ADD butter to skillet; add onions and sauté for 3 minutes. Add sherry, reduce by one-third. Add apricots, brown sugar, and parsley, blend well. Bring to a boil and simmer for 5 minutes. Add lamb chops back in at last minute to heat through before serving.

DIVIDE couscous and carrot patties between four or six warmed plates, add lamb chops and top with sauce and serve. *(Serves 4 to 6)*

> **WINE:** *Tempranillo (tested with a 2004 Campo Viejo Reseva) or a Rioja.*

Spicy Lamb Meatballs with Garlic Peanut Sauce Appetizer

2   jalapeno peppers, chopped *(1 pepper deseeded)*
4   large shallots
1   small yellow onion
6   garlic cloves
1   carrot, chopped
1   tablespoon turmeric in ½ cup bread crumbs
1   tablespoon fresh ginger slices
2   tablespoons tamarind, soaked with
    2 tablespoons water*
1   tablespoon brown sugar
2   tablespoons soy sauce
½   teaspoon cinnamon
3   pounds ground lamb

PREHEAT oven to 350°F. Non-stick spray baking pan with sides.

IN a food processor chop jalapenos, shallots, onion, garlic, carrot, turmeric and bread crumbs, ginger slices, tamarind, brown sugar, soy sauce and cinnamon. Add lamb and pulse until combined.

ROLL mixture into 1-inch meatballs; place on baking sheet. Bake 20-25 minutes, depending on size.

Garlic Peanut Sauce

    1 tablespoon butter
    2 shallots, finely diced
    3 garlic cloves, crushed
    ½ cup warm water
    2 tablespoons soy sauce
    5 tablespoons crunchy peanut butter
    1 teaspoon grated ginger
    1 teaspoon hot chili paste *(in a tube or jar)*

MELT the butter in a saucepan and add the shallots and garlic. Cook until soft, but not brown. Pour in the water, soy sauce, peanut butter, ginger and chili paste. Bring to a boil then simmer until thick, about 5-10 minutes. *(Serves many)*

WINE: *dry Riesling, white Burgundy. We had a Muller-Thurgau.*

*COOK'S NOTE Can substitute 2 tablespoons Tamarind paste for real tamarind, or 2 tablespoons lime juice and 1 tablespoon brown sugar.

Spicy Stir-Fried Sichuan Shredded Lamb with Soba Noodles

Thanks to my well-traveled step-daughter Julia, I have been able to enjoy fresh spices from Central America, India and now China. We encountered Sichuan peppercorns in the Hunan District of Beijing in December 2008. Don, step-daughter Em and I traveled to Beijing to spend the Christmas holidays with Julia, a Fulbright Scholar researching contemporary Buddhism in China. It was an eye-opening visit on so many levels. I have traveled throughout Europe, North Africa, Central and South America, many U.S. states, Virgin and West Indies Islands, and I have never been to a country where no one, except in the hospitality sector, speaks the English language.

We would have been lost if Julia did not speak and understand the language so well. It was so cool to get in a cab and listen to her carry on a conversation, joking and finally dickering when she felt we were being overcharged. What fun! Jules had our itinerary on yellow sticky notes framing her computer screen. It included temples, the Olympic Park, the Opera, Silk Street shopping, Starbuck's (thank goodness!), Christmas on The Great Wall, and of course my all-time favorite, an authentic Sichuan cooking class. Thanks Jules!

Black Sesame Kitchen is located in the Hunan District of Beijing. Traveling there, it really looks like the little side alleys you see in the movies. We had a bit of a difficult time finding the school. We finally ran into another lost student (who's been living there 6 years) and collectively called for them to meet us. It was not a place we would have found on our own.

This district is in the early stages of being gentrified, but heat is at a premium; the kitchen had opened the previous spring and hadn't been tested over a Beijing winter. Our room was not warm, except from the heat of the two woks in the front of the room. We all kept our layers of clothes on, fleece hats included, until it was our turn to cook. The two teaching chefs are well-known in China. The translator for the chef was very good at enforcing my stand of "I want to do it myself," when my turn came to try out the eggplant recipe.

The end to this long story is they gave us Sichaun peppercorns to bring back. You can buy them at The Spice House (see Resources), and they are the same intensity!

1½   pounds lamb, shoulder cut into thin shreds*
2   teaspoons soy sauce
1   egg white, lightly beaten
3   tablespoons canola oil
1   garlic clove, minced
1   tablespoon fresh ginger, peeled and grated or minced
1   teaspoon whole Sichuan peppercorns
2   Thai chilies, stemmed, seeded, and chopped,
    (or 1 teaspoon red pepper flakes)
1   cup shredded cabbage
1   tablespoon dry sherry
    salt to taste
½   pound soba noodles, cooked according to directions
1   scallion, trimmed and chopped, for garnish

COMBINE the lamb shreds with the soy sauce and egg white. Heat the oil in a wok or deep skillet over high heat. When the oil is almost smoking, stir in garlic, ginger, peppercorns, and chilies. Cook until fragrant, about 15 seconds. Add cabbage and cook 2 minutes.

STIR in lamb and cook until lightly browned.

ADD sherry and cooked noodles to lamb, combine garnish, and serve immediately. (*Serves 4*)

WINE: *chilled Pinot Noir, Riesling, or very cold Shipyard Summer or Export Ale.*

*COOK'S NOTE Freeze lamb for 30 minutes before cutting, it will be easier. This dish has great heat and aroma from the Thai chilies and flowery, smoky Sichuan peppercorns.

Wine Descriptions

The wines listed here are those recommended with the lamb dishes within this cookbook. It is not a complete list of all the countries, regions, districts, or varietals. The first list contains the varietals paired with the lamb dishes and second list contains the country, region and their predominate grapes.

As a general rule wines produced from new world countries such as U.S., Australia, Chili, Argentina, South Africa label their wines by varietal; the type of grape, which depending upon the country laws, account for at least 75% of the wine. Old world countries such as France, Italy, Spain, Lebanon and Portugal label their wines by the region within the country that the grapes were grown.

VARIETAL	DESCRIPTION
Aglianico	*medium to full-bodied, slightly smoky red*
Albarino	*medium-bodied briny white*
Barbera	*medium-bodied, high-acid, fruity red*
Blueberry	*full-bodied well balanced soft red Maine wine*
Cabernet Sauvignon	*full bodied red with large, firm tannins*
Chardonnay	*medium to full-bodied white, rich white wine*
Garganega	*light to medium-bodied delicate and silky finish*
Gewurztraminer	*medium-bodied white, very aromatic*
Gruner Veltliner	*medium-bodied white, fruity and peppery*
Malbec	*full-bodied red, rich in tannins with dried fruit, black currants and plum*
Mead	*dry white with honey aromas from Maine*
Merlot	*medium-bodied red with hints of berry, plum and currant*
Muller-Thurgau	*light -bodied white; described as cross between Riesling and Sylvaner*

VARIETAL	DESCRIPTION
Nebbiolo	*medium-bodied, similar to Pinot Noir*
Pinot Blanc	*medium-bodied white, similar to Chardonnay*
Pinot Gris	*light to medium-bodied, crisp and acidic white*
Pinot Noir	*light to full-bodied, a delicate and nuanced red*
Pinotage	*full-bodied red with spicy notes*
Primitivo	*full-bodied red similar to red Zinfandel*
Riesling	*light to full-bodied white, varying degrees of sweetness with fruit*
Sauvignon Blanc	*light to medium-bodied acidic white, sometimes grassy and citrusy*
Semillion	*medium-bodied white melon aromas*
Shiraz	*sparkling or still and ranging from dry to sweet, also known as Syrah*
Syrah	*full bodied red with black pepper finish also know as Shiraz*
Trebbiano	*medium-bodied red minerality with a crisp finish*
Viognier	*dry, floral, full-bodied white*
Vouvray	*medium-bodied dry to sweet white*
Zindandel	*medium to full-bodied red; typically, spicy, berry and pepper flavors*

COUNTRY	REGION	DISTRICT AND DESCRIPTIONS
FRANCE	**Provence**	*Bandol- medium to full-bodied red Mourvedre, Grenache, Cabernet Sauvignon and Syrah*
	Beaujolais	*light bodied red 100% Gamay*
	Bordeaux-red	*medium to full-bodied Cabernet Sauvignon and Merlot*
	Bordeaux-white	*light to medium-bodied Sauvignon Blanc and Semillion*
	Burgundy-red	*medium to full bodied 100% Pinot Noir*
	Burgundy-white	*medium to full-bodied 100% Chardonnay*
	Loire	*light to medium-bodied dry to sweet Sauvignon Blanc or Chenin Blanc*
	Rhone	*Chateauneuf du Pape-full-bodied red Grenache and Syrah*
	Rhone	*Hermitage- medium to full-bodied red 100% Syrah*
ITALY	**Tuscany**	*medium to full-bodied red Sangiovese, Cabernet Sauvignon and Merlot*
	Piedmont	*Barbaresco – medium to full-bodied red 100% Nebbiolo*
	Piedmont	*Barolo – medium to full-bodied red 100% Nebbiolo*
	Veneto	*Soave - light-bodied dry white Garganega and Trebbiano*
	Veneto	*Valpolicella - light-bodied red Corvina*

COUNTRY	REGION	DISTRICT AND DESCRIPTIONS
SPAIN	**Ribera Del Duero**	*medium to full-bodied Tempranillo and Cabernet Sauvignon*
	Rioja	*medium to full-bodied red Tempranillo*
LEBANON	**Baka Valley**	*Chateau Musar- medium-bodied red*

Sage and Bordeaux

Purveyors

This cookbook was created with the help of many hands; editor, testers and none more creative than the purveyors of specialty products whose personal pride in their products is an inspiration to cooks and wine connoisseurs everywhere.

BARTLETT MAINE ESTATE WINERY & SPIRITS OF MAINE DISTILLERY
Kathe and Bob Bartlett
175 Chicken Mill Rd.
Gouldsboro, ME 04607
(207)546-2408
www.bartlettwinery.com
—*World renowned wines and spirits from local fruit since 1983*

CELLARDOOR VINEYARD
Bettina Doulton
367 Youngtown Road
Lincolnville, ME 04849
(207)763-4478
www.mainewine.com
—*Enjoy our wines and savor your visit!*

DRAGONFLY FARM & WINERY
Todd & Treena Nadeau
1069 Mullen Road
Stetson, ME 04488
www.mainewinegrower.com
—*All wines are produced from grapes and berries grown and hand-picked in Maine by the Nadeau Family.*

MAINE GOODIES
George and Terri Stone
5 Winslow Road
Albion, ME 04910
www.mainegoodies.com
(866)385-6238
(888)203-8471
—*All great Maine products*

RAYE'S MUSTARD MILL
Karen and Kevin Raye
PO Box 2
Eastport, ME 04631
(800)853-1903
www.rayesmustard.com
—*America's only remaining
authentic stone-ground
mustard mill!*

SAWYER'S SPECIALTIES
Scott Worcester
353 Main Street
Southwest Harbor, ME 04679
(207)244-3317
—*wine and cheese specialty shop*

SHIPYARD BREWING COMPANY
86 Newbury Street
Portland, ME 04101
1-800-BREW-ALE
www.shipyard.com
—*Enjoy Maine's #1 Micro Brew*

SUNSET ACRES FARM AND DAIRY
Bob Bowen and Anne Bossi
769 Bagaduce Road
Brooksville, ME 04617
(207)326-4741
www.sunsetacresfarm.com
—*Goat milk and cheese, free
range eggs, meats and poultry*

SWEET ENERGY
Tim Ziter
195 Acorn Lane
Colchester, VT 05446
(802)655-1372
www.sweetenergy.com
—*Premier dried fruits, gourmet
nuts, preserves, decadent choco-
late and more.*

THE SPICE HOUSE
Tom and Patty Penzy Erd
1512 North Wells Street
Chicago, IL 60610
(312)274-0378
www.thespicehouse.com
—*I buy almost all my spices and
herbs that I don't grow, from
Patty!*